M.R.N.

Our Cultures

edited by

MARILYN MARQUIS **and** SARAH NIELSEN

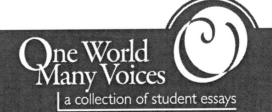

One World
Many Voices

a collection of student essays

One World Many Voices: Our Cultures
Copyright © 2010 by Marilyn Marquis and Sarah Nielsen

All rights reserved.

Published in the United States and the United Kingdom
by WingSpan Press, Livermore, CA

The WingSpan name, logo and colophon are the trademarks of
WingSpan Publishing.

ISBN 978-1-59594-411-5

First edition 2010

Printed in the United States of America

www.wingspanpress.com

Library of Congress Control Number 2010930630

1 2 3 4 5 6 7 8 9 10

This collection of essays, *Our Cultures*, about family, religious, and national cultures, is the first book in *One World Many Voices*, a series of collected essays written by and for English language learners. The series stems from an effort to provide easy and interesting extensive reading material for students in the ESL program at Las Positas College, in Livermore, California.

The editors of this series initiated READERS WRITING FOR READERS in 2006 to encourage students to write for readers who are learning English. By participating in READERS WRITING FOR READERS and reading the resulting books, students have the powerful experience of learning from peers and of helping others with their language development. Knowledge comes from students themselves. In reading the writing of their peers, students may simultaneously join a community of readers, discover themselves in the experiences of others, and expand their understanding of the world.

These student-generated essays, edited to control the variety of sentence structure and the range of vocabulary, provide beginning level students with interesting, easy to understand material that they can read successfully without the use of a dictionary.

We wish to extend our thanks to the ESL faculty at Las Positas College for engaging their students in READERS WRITING FOR READERS. We are deeply grateful to the students for their genuine and creative contributions.

Marilyn Marquis and Sarah Nielsen, editors

Acknowledgements

*W*E ARE INDEBTED TO THE students in the English as a Second Language program at Las Positas College for their enthusiastic participation in READERS WRITING FOR READERS. Their heartfelt writing about their lives, their feelings, their families, their customs, and their struggles with living in a new country has inspired us to create this series of student-generated essays for their extensive reading.

We also want to acknowledge the many others who have contributed to this series. Fredda Cassidy and the faculty and students in the Visual Communications program at Las Positas College worked patiently with us to establish the look and feel of these books. They designed the layout, logo, and covers through a truly collaborative process, in particular Linda Roberts, Rebecca Schoefer, Melinda Bandler, and Meg Epperly. Thank you!

Thank you also to the instructors in the English as a Second Language program at Las Positas College for inviting us into their classrooms to present READERS WRITING FOR READERS to their students and for encouraging their students to participate in the project.

We would like to acknowledge the contributions of individuals who offered feedback, suggestions, proofreading, and support with special thanks to Dr. Philip Manwell, Dean of Arts and Communications at Las Positas College.

Table of
Contents

Differences

 # Differences

Not Too Difficult Now

FATIMA ALI

*W*HEN WE FIRST CAME TO the United States in June 2000, my life was very difficult. I was a single mom. I didn't speak English. I didn't have a car. I couldn't even buy groceries. This was not a good start for a new immigrant. After a couple of years, my children and I learned English, and my life gradually became easier. When my husband returned to our family, we had another change to a happier life. I learned how to drive. I got my driver license. I finally bought a car. Now I can buy groceries. I can also come to the college for ESL classes.

Three Differences

YE JEONG CHOI

My COUNTRY, KOREA, IS DIFFERENT from the United States in some very interesting ways. For example, when people say hello in Korea, they respectfully bow their heads. When people say hello in America, most people wave their hand. Also when a person bumps against another person by accident in public, most Korean people don't say, "Sorry," or "Excuse me." Americans usually do. I like this simple way of showing good manners.

Another thing that is different concerns food. Korean food is much more spicy. Korean people like spicy food, but American people generally don't like spicy food. Americans on the contrary like oily food. The food in the United States is more oily than Korean food. It is difficult for me to eat some American food.

One additional difference between these two cultures relates to attitude. It seems to me that most Koreans are impatient. Americans live in contentment, and they are patient. I don't know why this is different. I observed it very often. Koreans usually say, "Hurry up. Hurry up," and they move quickly. But Americans don't seem to be in a hurry. They are patient and calm. This is sometimes difficult because I am impatient. I am not able to cure my impatience, but I will try. It is the way in America. I learned to appreciate these differences.

Living Alone

JUAN LUNA CRUZ

In 1995, MY FAMILY AND I recognized the need for change. We had lots of interesting ideas, but no real plan yet. My wife and mother discussed many options, but they didn't talk to me about all of them. One day, my wife and mother talked to me. They asked if I wanted to work in a different place. I said that I was open to new ideas. At the time, I didn't think very much about it. I certainly didn't think of leaving the country. A couple of hours later, my wife and mother gave me a one-way ticket to travel to the USA. The next day, I was here. They planned this for a long time without telling me.

At first, I thought I was in a bad dream. Nobody knew me here. I did not have my wife and son; I missed them so much every day. I didn't know where to find a job, where to eat, or where to live. I eventually figured it all out, but I never really liked living alone. That was a big problem for four years.

Now, my days in the USA are different. I like the public services. I can work to support my family and continue studying to realize my dream of a happy future. I have learned to appreciate the style of living. Here everyone can help each other in the community.

Getting Used to the Weather

CRISTIANE FERREIRA-EDGETT

I MOVED TO THE UNITED STATES from Brazil in 2007 to marry my fiancée. I did not know what to expect. I worried about the transition from one language and culture to another. From my first day, I had to live in American culture and speak an uncomfortable language. I imagined some differences in advance, but not everything.

I arrived at the airport in Miami after a long flight. I really wanted a good cup of coffee. I went to an inviting coffee shop called Starbucks. I wanted a caramel latte. I could not understand the barista, and he could not understand me. I felt very confused and frustrated. Back then, I thought my language skills were good. I studied English for six years in Brazil. At that moment, I could not buy a cup of coffee. I had some work to do. I did not want language to make my life miserable.

I arrived in Miami during the summer. The weather felt like my hometown, Rio de Janeiro, so I felt comfortable. I thought the weather would be like that all year, like in Brazil. I was wrong there, too. After a couple of months, the weather started to get cold. Then I began to feel homesick and a little depressed. I don't know why the weather made me homesick. On the bright side, I bought a lot of new clothes, and a space heater.

My adaptation to life in the United States was not so easy. After two years, my English is much better, and I am totally used to the weather.

So Many Changes

ANONYMOUS

LIVING IN THE USA CHANGED my life. First of all, living here helped me get a good education. In Afghanistan, I was about to start school, but the Taliban came into power and closed schools for girls. So, I never went to school in my country. Now, I am going to college here. Living in the USA helped me become bilingual, too. In Afghanistan, I couldn't speak any English. I only spoke my first language, Dari. Now in the USA, I speak English most of the time. This new language helped me get a good job in the USA. Living here also changed some of my habits. In Afghanistan, I always wore a *shal war kamse*, a long shirt over pants. Now in the USA, I wear jeans and a top. I also wear different clothes when I go out. Back in Afghanistan, when I left the house, I wore a garment called a *hajdb* (a long black robe) with a scarf that covered much of my face. Girls were not allowed to wear makeup either. Now I can wear shorter clothes and even makeup, if I want to. In Afghanistan, I was not allowed to talk to boys, but in the USA, I can talk with anyone I want to. Coming to the USA changed my life a lot!

Driving

GAHYOUNG (JUDY) KIM

THE MOST DISTINCT DIFFERENCE BETWEEN my country, Korea, and the United Sstates is driving. Everyone here drives a car. In Korea, many people, even professional people, do not drive. Korea has a good transportation system. I was surprised when I arrived. I needed to learn to drive because I wanted a comfortable life in the United States. For example, I wanted to go to the store, but I had to spend more than half an hour to get there. So, I reluctantly learned to drive. I also learned how to control my nerves while I was driving. At first I was terribly afraid and nervous. My husband was my first driving teacher. Perhaps this was not such a good idea. While I was learning to drive, I was also crying and fighting with my husband. Every driving lesson was a living hell.

Now all that is passed, and I can drive comfortably. I can drive my children to school, drive to work, and drive to the college for ESL classes. Living in the United States is living behind the wheel. Now I have a comfortable life.

Dating
ANONYMOUS

IN AMERICA, PEOPLE HAVE FREEDOM to have a boyfriend or girlfriend. They have freedom to go on dates. They can have romantic relationships when they are in high school. Boys and girls go to dances and parties together. The parents allow young people to have relationships, but they do not really need permission from their parents to have a girlfriend or boyfriend. After the age of eighteen, young people can even live by themselves. Americans can marry someone from another country with no problems from their family. Parents in the United States give their children a lot of freedom for choosing girlfriends and boyfriends. This is all very different from Afghanistan.

In Afghanistan, the girls and boys cannot have a girlfriend or boyfriend when they are young. They cannot have a date with someone unless they are engaged. Parents must give their permission for every part of the relationship. Some families are very strict with these rules. For example, I am engaged to a man, but we do not know each other in person. I can see him on Webcam, and we talk on the phone or with a computer. He lives in Germany, and I live in the US. This is fine with me. Since childhood, this is my expectation. Parents choose the spouse for their children. They check on the family history and make sure it is a good match.

The ideas about romance are very different in these two cultures.

Discrimination and Opportunities

ALBERTINA MBACHI

THREE THINGS ARE ESPECIALLY DIFFICULT for me living in the USA: the weather, the neighborhoods, and discrimination. I worry most about discrimination. Before I first came to the United States, I didn't experience any discrimination. One day, my son saw a classmate and wanted to play with him. My son was very sad because his classmate's mother said that he couldn't play with her son. I was also not welcome in her house. I felt really hurt by this, and I missed my own country. There is no separation among people there. Now, though, I don't worry about this neighbor. I only hope that she will forget about the color of my child's skin and let him play with her son.

The difficulties of living in the USA are balanced by many interesting things. There are many things to love about this country. It is easy to find a job. There are many, many opportunities. They are limited only by what you dream for yourself. If my own country had these possibilities, I might not live in the USA.

The Difficult Will Become Easy
HYUN SUE PAK

THERE ARE MANY DIFFICULT THINGS about living in the USA. I came to America seven years ago. I didn't speak English very well, and many things about the culture were unfamiliar to me. So, I couldn't find a job. There are many people from different countries in the United States. They have to take dirty jobs and hard jobs because they cannot speak English very well. I was one of those people. Now, I want to speak English well. Then I can find a good job. I hope that difficult things will become easy for me.

American culture is more comfortable for me now. There are some things that I especially like, particularly the way that the disabled are treated. The U.S. has facilities for disabled people everywhere. For example, there are special features in public restrooms, access to restaurants, ramps into buildings, special parking spaces in parking lots, and ramps on every sidewalk. I like that. There are more facilities for disabled people here than in my country, Korea.

Some Surprises

JU YEON PARK

I MOVED TO THE UNITED STATES three years ago. Now I feel more comfortable with the many differences between this country and Korea. Some of those differences were quite surprising at first. For example, I went to the DMV to get a driver license. There were a lot of people, so I took a number and waited three hours. I never waited for over one hour in a public place in Korea. I was very upset and got angry. It is still difficult for me to be patient in a public place. Now I know about the DMV. Their long lines are unique.

I especially like the treatment of disabled people in the United States. I sometimes see disabled people in the shopping malls or buying groceries. It is unbelievable that disabled people can go outdoors by themselves. In my country, Korea, disabled people stay home or in special schools or homes. Many people ignore or reject them in public. Most Americans are thoughtful to disabled people.

The Difficult Times Are Over

MUNISA ABDUL RAUF

*W*HEN I FIRST CAME TO the USA, I faced some difficulties. First of all, there was the language. I could not speak English, so I couldn't find a job. I couldn't ask for directions or communicate about other topics, either. I also couldn't drive. I was stuck. I could not go anywhere. Fortunately, all the difficult times are over.

I like the educational system the best. My children go to a good school. The teachers are kind, and the teaching methods are up-to-date. This country also has beautiful scenery and freedom for all people. Compared to life in my home country, my life in the United States is more comfortable. My family and I like living in the USA.

Hard Times and Good Neighbors
MARY ROBLES

FOR ME, LIVING IN THE USA is very difficult because I don't speak English well. Speaking English is very stressful. I am working on my English, though, by taking English classes at the local college. I also practice with my neighbors and my husband. I listen to music with English lyrics, and I read books and newspapers in English. When my language skills get better, I want to find a good job.

The language is difficult, but I like living in the United States. The people are so good. My neighbors, for example, are friendly and kind. They always spend time with our family. When my son had surgery, they helped me take care of him. I am grateful for their care and attention. I hope we will be friends forever.

My Life

LAILA SANCHEZ

⟨A⟩T FIRST, LEARNING THE LANGUAGE, the culture, and the customs of the United States were all difficult. These things are still difficult. It was also difficult to withdraw from my family in Mexico. I wanted to start a different life in America, but it was not easy. Some things are still a struggle. One surprise was the racism against Latinos in this country. Those difficulties are always there, but there are many things I especially appreciate. I like learning a second language. I like better opportunities in this country. I like living with more safety rules and more respect. I like working and earning my own money. I like having friends from many different countries. I like having friends of many different nationalities. Most of all, I like the fact that people can come to this country from anywhere in the world. Everyone can have an opportunity to study and have a better life. I changed as a person, and I like that, too. I gradually learned more about my second language, English. I will have a good job and a happy future. I can achieve my goals.

What Do You Like Best?

JIN-CHOI YOUNG

I CAME TO THE UNITED STATES five months ago. I can already tell that living here is fun and exciting. First of all, the environment in California makes me happy. The clear, fresh air always makes me feel good. I rarely stay inside. I go outside for a deep breath of air. Everyplace I go in California, I feel that it is like heaven. Whether I am breathing the air of the Tri-Valley or that of Lake Tahoe, I feel refreshed. This is a great place. My friendly neighbors are also very special. One day, I was out in my neighborhood and needed to find a restroom. My English was horrible at that time. I saw a man doing his daily exercises. I approached him for help in locating a restroom. He stopped running and kindly pointed out the restroom to me. He showed me where to go. I also love the open education system. For example, Las Positas College has a good ESL program for international students. All of the ESL instructors are hard workers and always help their students succeed. My instructor carefully checks my homework and comments on my writing assignments. Living in the United States is exciting and interesting. Living here helped me realize happiness.

CHAPTER TWO
Unique Traditions

Unique Traditions

Henna

SABILA ASIF

*T*HE ART OF HENNA IS a very popular cultural tradition in Pakistan. We use henna tattoos for celebrations like Eid festivals, wedding ceremonies, and birth celebrations. Henna tattoos are connected to good luck and good fortune. This tradition is very old, thousands of years old. Henna is a dye. It is usually applied to the hands and feet as decoration. Sometimes it is on the arms and neck. These henna tattoos are popular in many countries including Afghanistan, India, and Egypt. The Urdu name is *mehndi*.

Henna comes from a tree that grows in hot regions like India, Pakistan, and North Africa. The dye comes from the leaves of the tree. First, people dry the leaves and stems, and then they grind them up. Next, they make a paste. This paste makes temporary tattoos. The traditions of henna are typically passed down from mother to daughter, from one generation to the next. Women enjoy creating tattoos for each other. Special artists create beautiful designs and then make a stencil for people to copy. The designs are very delicate and beautiful.

In Pakistan, traditionally henna was for women, but now it can be for men, too. For very special occasions, like a wedding, both the bride and the groom have henna. Henna is a symbol of love between husband and wife.

If you see a woman with henna tattoos on her hands and feet, you will know she was celebrating some special event with her family and friends.

Hah-Hoe Tall
SUNG KYUN KIM

MASKS AS FOLK ART ARE popular around the world, not only in Korea. The representative masks of Korea come from a particular village, Hah-Hoe. We have many different kinds of masks in Korea, but the masks from this village are our precious cultural inheritance. These masks became a national treasure in 1964. They are masterpieces of the world of art. They show the originality and artistic traits of Korea.

In early times in Korea, people made these masks to chase away the bad ghosts. They made masks in scary shapes. Some were in the shapes of gods. As time passed, the ideas about the masks and ghosts changed. Through the years, the masks became part of traditional plays. The plays offered a judgment on the social and cultural customs of Korea at that time. It was a judgment about the royal class and a judgment about the separation of men and women.

The most popular play is *Hah-Hoe Byullshin-Goot Nori*. *Nori* means play in Korean.

People made the traditional masks from paper or from a gourd. After the play, they burned the masks and threw them away. Therefore, it is impossible to find any of those old masks. In Hah-Hoe village, the masks were made of wood. Each mask was stored and kept safe. Consequently, we have the masks from that village. These are called Hah-Hoe Tall.

These masks are very important to Korean culture. They are a rare example of old traditional Korean culture. These masks rank among the most beautiful in the world of traditional folk art.

The masks look very much like Korean people. They have the same facial characteristics and skin color, but the other colors are all unique. Ancient people carved the masks from *paulownia coreana* trees. Then they painted the faces and covered them with lacquer. There are eleven masks in the collection. Each one represents a different type of person. For example, there is an aristocrat, a monk, a butcher, and a scholar. The faces look like people, but each side of the face is a little different. Each delicate mask has a separate chin. Also, the chin connects to the mask with string. This allows the actors in the play to express emotions and ideas differently.

These masks are a very important part of Korean culture. They connect the modern world to the ancient world. They reveal the superior craftsmanship of our historical artists. They also connect to the spirit of the people. This is a spirit of freedom and equality. They show the hope for a world where life is respected.

Polite Language
ANONYMOUS

THE KOREAN LANGUAGE IS INTERESTING and unique. It has different levels of formality. This makes it difficult for people to learn the language. Many languages have formal and informal language. Even English has formal and informal language. Korean has more levels than other languages. It has seven levels, and each level has special word endings to show respect to the listener. The verb in the sentence shows the level of formality. Koreans must learn the formal forms, and they must learn when to use each form. Sometimes this is difficult and confusing. We use the most formal forms to talk to an older person or for a first conversation with a person. When we meet someone, we always use polite language. If someone uses the informal forms of Korean on a first meeting, it will seem rude and ill-mannered. After we know a person well, we use the comfortable level of formality. The formal form is also important for talking to someone who has a high rank. For example, when I was in the army, I used the formal forms to talk to any soldier with a higher rank. In the family, we use the intimate form to talk to our parents when we are young. As we get older, we use formal language to talk to our parents and our grandparents. This makes the Korean language unique and very different from English.

Children's Folk Art Toys
ANONYMOUS

IN TAIWAN, TRADITIONAL FOLK ART is very important. Visitors can learn about Taiwanese culture and history from the folk art. Of course, folk art includes many things, such as cloth and basket weaving, masks, cooking utensils, and children's toys. These are all items that people make for a useful purpose, but they make them in a special way. They are often beautiful. Over a long time, these things begin to represent the culture. Many of the Taiwanese traditional folk art comes from Chinese culture.

When I was a child in Taiwan, I played with some traditional folk art toys. My favorite was the bamboo dragonfly. This is an old Chinese toy. It is very simple. It has a stick and a propeller. Children love to watch the dragonfly float into the air after they spin it in their hands first. Anyone can do it. Just hold the stick against one hand, and roll it with the other hand. The propeller will begin to spin. Once it spins fast, it will fly in the air.

Another traditional toy from ancient China is the *ocarina*. This is a small musical instrument. It fits comfortably in a child's hand. It is made of pottery. It has a round shape with a little place to blow air into it. It also has holes for fingers to cover. Each hole will make a different musical note. Children enjoy making music with these little toy instruments.

The art of paper sculpture is very old in Taiwan. Artists can make beautiful paper flowers, fish, trees, and nature scenes. These Taiwanese artists make sculptures, but with paper. These are three-dimensional forms. They are delicate and very beautiful. Children also learn to make simple paper sculptures at school.

Children in Taiwan also learn to make Chinese knots. This is a special technique to make a beautiful design from a single piece of rope or ribbon. The art of tying knots is very ancient in China, and it has a special charm. These knots create lucky patterns and have special meaning. Children can learn to make some simple knot pattern designs when they are young.

Folk art is a very important part of Taiwanese culture. It shows the beauty of Chinese culture. Traditional folk art is our important treasure over many generations.

Our Fishermen's Odd Tradition

TAI NGUYEN

VIETNAM IS A VERY OLD country, and our traditions and customs are also very old. Some of the traditions are not popular throughout the country. Some are special for only a small group of people. I learned about an odd, but interesting, tradition of fishermen when I was a child.

In this tradition, on a boat or a ship, no one turns over a fish while they are eating it. Fishermen in Vietnam believe this is bad luck. If someone turns a fish over during a meal on a boat or ship, the boat or ship will sink. In Vietnam, people clean each fish, but they do not remove the bone. When people eat the fish, they eat from one side, then turn the fish over to eat from the other side. But no one can do this on a boat or a ship. Instead, after they eat from one side of the fish, they remove the bone, and then they eat the rest of the fish.

When I was twelve years old, a friend invited me to her home. She lived in Long Hai in the eastern part of the country. Many people there earn their living from fishing. My friend's father is a fisherman. He owns a ship. One evening, we went fishing at sea. Before we left, her mother prepared a meal for us. Late in the evening, we all felt hungry. We began to eat the fish dinner from her mother. I did not know about the tradition of never turning over the fish, but I learned quickly. I started to turn the fish over after we finished one side. Her father stopped me very boldly. I felt scared at first. When he saw my face, he smiled. He slowly removed the bone and told me about this custom. He warned me to be very careful about this in the future.

Later that night, her father told us many stories. He heard these stories from other fishermen. All of the stories told about boats and ships sinking after someone turned over a fish during a meal. I believed these stories because I was young. I always avoided turning over a fish because I did not want anyone to die. One day, when I was older, I was in a restaurant on a big ship. I saw people turn the fish over as they ate. I was worried, but then nothing happened. I am still alive and writing about this now. So I no longer believe the stories from my friend's father.

Still, when I am in Vietnam on a boat or ship, I never turn the fish over. After I finish eating one side, I always remove the bone and then continue eating. That is the tradition. I hope you will follow this tradition if you visit Vietnam.

10/21/16

The Day of Making Kimchi

ANONYMOUS

HEALTH MAGAZINE NAMED KOREA'S TRADITIONAL food, *kimchi*, one of the world's most healthy foods. We eat it because it tastes delicious. It is also good for preventing cancer and other diseases because it has many vitamins and fiber. The most well known *kimchi* is cabbage *kimchi*, but we can use different vegetables to make it. No one in Korea could imagine life without *kimchi* for breakfast, lunch, and dinner. That is the reason for our special day for making *kimchi*. When winter approaches, Koreans prepare to make *kimchi* to eat during the winter.

The day for making *kimchi* was the most exciting day for me when I was a child. Before the special day, my mother went shopping to buy all of the ingredients. After shopping, she was very busy. She washed the cabbage, radishes, onions, garlic, ginger and other vegetables. She soaked the cabbage in salt overnight. This is a very important step. While the cabbage soaked, my mother, brother, sister, and I cut the onions and pounded garlic and ginger in a small mortar. We shredded the radishes into long thin strips. We talked while we worked. We talked about school and friends. We told funny stories to each other. We went to bed tired. We also knew about the work for tomorrow.

Early the next morning, my mother prepared the ingredients for the day. She prepared the seasonings: salt, *saewoo jeot,* or *meyolchi jeot. Jeot* is a kind of fish. The fish is soaked in salt water. She also set out chili pepper and sugar.

Later, friends and neighbors came to our house to make *kimchi* with us. We needed a lot of people to make *kimchi* for the winter. This made the day very exciting. We worked for half of the day to make enough *kimchi*. When we finished, we ate a delicious lunch with delicious *kimchi*, of course. Then we put the *kimchi* in jars.

My father was busy outside while we worked in the kitchen. He dug a big hole. This is an important step in the process of making *kimchi*. The jars of *kimchi* sat under the ground in the hole for a week. It fermented in the ground. The fermenting preserved the *kimchi* so we could eat it all winter.

These days, it is much easier to make *kimchi*. We do not need to make enough for the entire winter now. But many Korean families keep the traditional day for making *kimchi*. This is an important family day in Korean culture.

Family Culture, Lovely Thursday
FRANCISCA RIVERA

EVERY THURSDAY NIGHT IS TIME for our family. Several years ago we were having problems finding the right time to communicate. There was never time for our family. We tried different ways to set up time. We went out to eat, visited the parks, and tried many more ways, but nothing worked, not even Friday nights. So, my husband came up with the idea for Thursday night. This worked well for our family. Now Thursday night is time to talk as a family. During the week, we each make notes about something that we didn't like about the week. We listen to each other's concerns. As parents, we give the children our best advice or answer their questions. Sometimes we have problems from school to solve. Sometimes there are problems with friends. This is a good way for us to communicate. We open our hearts and our minds for each other. After dinner, sometimes we watch a movie together. Then we can talk about the movie together. This is our family tradition, and we all like it very much.

Heredia's Family Weekend

GABRIELA ORENDAIN

IN MY MOM'S FAMILY, WE have a very nice tradition. Every year on the last weekend of August, all of the members of my mother's family come to our city, Guadalajara, Jalisco, Mexico. People come from all over the country to celebrate the Heredia's family traditional weekend gathering. Some people fly in for the celebration, but most people live in the city. It really is a very important celebration, and we all come to have a good time. We have some important traditions for the weekend.

Everyone must be a blood relative. No one can invite a friend. In addition, when someone comes for the first time, a family member must introduce the person to all of us. It is fun to see if the new person can remember all of the names. Also, each family must organize a game for the children and adults. They must bring all the necessary things to play the game, show the rules of the game, and supervise the play. Some people try to bring new and original games for everyone to play.

After the games, we gather for dinner. Each family brings food, and we all share it. Finally it is time to dance. Someone always brings music for dancing. The sounds of laughter and giggling on the dance floor always makes us happy. We always stay very late and enjoy as much fun with our family as we can on this special weekend.

CHAPTER THREE
Wedding Customs

Weddings in my Family
Engagement and Marriage
Traditional Pakistani Marriage
An Iranian Tradition
Weddings in India
Wedding Celebrations in Serbia
The Polish Wedding Ceremony
Ethiopian Orthodox Marriage Ceremony

Wedding Customs

Weddings in My Family

MARILYN MARQUIS

ARRIAGE TRADITIONS CHANGED A LOT between 1939 and 2003. My mother lived at home with her family until she got married. It was unusual for a woman to live away from her family before marriage. She met my father at a church picnic when she was twenty-four years old. They dated for a year before the wedding. A traditional church wedding was very important to both of them and to their families. There were a lot of people at my parents' wedding. My mother had nine sisters and three brothers. She worked and sang in a woman's chorus, so she also had many friends. My father had a smaller family, but he, too, had many friends. As a child, I always enjoyed looking at my parents' wedding photo album. There are pictures of my parents in church, walking out of church with happy faces, dancing together, eating dinner, and cutting the wedding cake. My mother had to stand on a chair to cut the cake because it had seven layers. A glass wedding couple sat on top of the cake. My mother's mother made her beautiful white wedding gown. Mother kept her wedding gown in a wooden chest in her room. I loved to open the wooden chest to look at my mother's treasures. Her wedding dress was the most special treasure in that chest. My own daughters also enjoyed looking at grandma's treasures.

In 1992, my older daughter got married, and she wore her grandmother's beautiful white wedding gown. Like her grandmother, she was twenty-five. She had a very traditional church wedding. Some of the pictures of her wedding are very much like those at my parents' wedding. There are pictures of the bride and groom at the altar in church, walking out of church with happy smiles, dancing together, eating dinner, and cutting the wedding cake.

My parents' wedding and my daughter's wedding looked very similar. They were also different in many ways. One difference was choice. My daughter chose where to get married and made all of the decisions about her wedding with her husband. The bride and groom decided where and when to get married. My daughter's boyfriend did not ask for permission to marry my daughter. Tradition was not a requirement.

In 2003, my younger daughter got married. She created her own traditions. She and her boyfriend lived in Washington DC, a long distance from both families. They did not want a traditional wedding in a church. They got married in a garden with close family and friends gathered around them. The bride wore a beautiful gown, but not a traditional white wedding gown. Their wedding cake had her grandparents' glass wedding couple on top.

Both of my daughters married wonderful young men. They each planned their own beautiful wedding.

The weddings were very different from each other. Both daughters included something from my parents' wedding. This pleased me.

Today in the United States, weddings can all be very different. In each wedding, a young couple in love makes a promise to each other in the presence of their families and friends. Weddings are always happy occasions.

Engagement and Marriage
ANONYMOUS

In AFGHANISTAN, WE HAVE A small party for the bride-to-be before the wedding. It is just for the women and girls. The groom's mother brings the henna bowl and special henna items to the bride's house. In the evening after the dinner, women and girls dance around the bowl of henna. The bowl is on a very beautifully decorated tray. The bride's family serves tea and desert for them. After that, seven unmarried girls put the henna on the bride's hands. They decorate her hands with beautiful designs. The tradition is important for the relationship of women.

On the wedding day in the morning, the bride and some of her close relatives go to the beauty parlor. They prepare their hair and makeup and get ready for the wedding. When the bride is ready, the groom goes to the beauty parlor. He takes her hand, and they go to the wedding hall together. Many people are there already. The families and friends begin to gather in the hall in the late afternoon. When the bride and the groom arrive at the wedding hall, the band plays the wedding song. The bride and the groom enter the hall very slowly. They walk step by step to their seats. The bride and groom sit in their seats to watch the dancing. The band plays favorite songs, and everyone dances. The bride and the groom watch them from their seats.

Then the ceremony begins. The mullah performs the ceremony. He asks the groom and the bride if they want to get married. They both say yes. Then he marries them. At the ceremony, the bride wears a green gown. It is tradition in our country. After the ceremony, a dinner is served. The bride changes her clothes before dinner. She wears a white gown for the reception. Everyone enjoys dinner and dancing. Then the bride and the groom cut the cake and serve it to each other. The guests dance for them. Some guests give gifts to the bride, and they take a photo with her. At the end of the party, the bride and the groom stand at the exit and thank everyone for their gifts and for coming to the party. Finally, the bride and groom go home to begin their new life.

Traditional Pakistani Marriage

ANONYMOUS

WEDDINGS ARE VERY IMPORTANT IN Pakistani culture. The wedding celebration continues for one week with four major ceremonies on four different days. From the first day, Mehndi, the bride and groom cannot see each other during the day. The bride and groom each have a ceremony, but they are not together. Each ceremony begins with a reading from the holy Quran. Green and yellow are the traditional colors for this day. Everyone wears these colors, including the bride. The bride also wears jewelry made from red roses and white jasmine. The bride cannot wear any makeup on this day. The groom wears traditional clothes, *shalwaar* and *kamees*. He also does not shave on this day or on any day until the wedding day. Friends and family of the groom bring sweets, flowers, and henna for the bride and the bride's family. The bride's family does the same thing for the groom. Finally, friends bring the bride and groom together under a decorated *dupatta*, or shawl, for the ceremony. They make beautiful designs on their hands with henna. They sing traditional songs during the ceremony. In some families, everyone dances. In other families, the men leave when the women dance.

The second important day is the bride's reception, *shaadi*. This event is at the bride's house or in a special hall. The bride's family prepares the reception. At this time, they give everything to the bride and groom to set up their house. This includes furniture, dishes, and bedding. This is the dowry. It always depends upon the finances of the bride's family. They also offer gifts to the groom and his family. This is called *salami*. The groom arrives at the reception with his family. It is the custom for the bride's sister and friends to try to block the groom and his friends from entering. They offer cash to the women, and then they can come in. This is always a fun part of the ceremony.

The third important step is Nikah. This is the Islamic marriage contract ceremony. It can take place at the bride's house before the marriage day. The *imam* performs the ceremony. The bride and groom each have two witnesses. The bride and groom leave together. Someone holds the holy Quran, over the bride and groom as they walk past. This is when the bride says goodbye to her parents and her siblings.

The final day of the wedding is Walima. This is the groom's reception. His parents make the arrangements for this ceremony. Most of the guests are the groom's relatives and friends. Some of the bride's friends and family are invited, too. The bride wears a beautifully decorated dress. She also wears jewelry from the groom's family. The groom usually wears a western style suit to this reception. They all enjoy a delicious dinner with traditional foods. After dinner, everyone dances along with the bride and groom.

An Iranian Tradition

KISIA

THERE IS A COMMON WEDDING tradition among Iranians. It is called *aghd*, the legal process of marriage. For this, the bride and groom sign a marriage certificate. This ceremony usually takes place at the bride's parents' house in a special room. The bride's parents prepare the room in a special way. Sometimes a professional decorator helps with the preparations. They put a spread on the floor, the *Sofre Aghd*. The spread is decorated with flowers. The colors of flowers match the items on the wedding spread. For example, my wedding room had red roses and white flowers. Green leaves hung from the walls and ceiling. Along each side of the spread, there were six bouquets of flowers in two rows. The white, red, and green flowers looked beautiful with the silver items on the spread. The spread is usually made from expensive fabric such as Termeh, a handmade Iranian fabric, or silk. Then different objects are placed on the spread. Each one symbolizes something unique in our culture.

Two special objects are candle holders and a mirror. The mirror sits between the two candle holders. A mirror is a symbol of light. A candle is a sign of fire. Both light and fire were important elements in ancient Iran. The couple keeps the mirror and candle holders throughout their marriage. Many couples pass these things on to their own daughter for her wedding. When the couple enters the room, they sit in front of the mirror. The bride has lace covering her face. Then the groom removes the lace. They see the reflection of their faces in the mirror. This brings honesty to their lives.

The spread also has many other items. Traditional flat bread is decorated with saffron, cinnamon, fresh herbs, and feta cheese, to bring happiness for the new couple. This symbolizes abundance and blessing. A bowl of crystallized sugar is a symbol of a sweet life. One basket has decorated almonds, walnuts, and hazelnuts in shells. Another basket has eggs, plain or painted, to symbolize fertility. Apples are a sign of human creation. A bowl of golden coins is a sign of wealth and prosperity. A bowl of raw rice symbolizes abundance. A bowl of salt will blind the evil eye, keeping bad luck away. Wild rye symbolizes continued good health and good luck. There is a cup of honey on the spread. After the marriage ceremony, the bride and groom each dip one finger in the cup of honey. Then they feed it to each other with hope for a sweet life.

Finally, a copy of the couple's holy book, the Quran, is on the spread. This is a symbol of God's blessing for the couple. Some couples use a poetry book instead of a religious book.

Aghd usually takes place in the early afternoon with close relatives and the couple's friends. The wedding spread remains in place all night long. Attendants visit it and take pictures beside the spread. *Sofre Aghd* is a unique and spectacular part of the Iranian wedding celebration.

Weddings in India
PUSHPINDER SINGH

MARRIAGE IS IMPORTANT IN EVERY culture. Everyone hopes to find a true love and have a happy life. Each culture has a different way of helping young people find the perfect mate. In India, marriage is different from the United States. Our parents often participate in the decision about a marriage partner.

In some cases, the parents choose the marriage partner. The parents make an agreement with other parents for their children to marry in the future. The children are still babies at the time. Often, the children never meet each other until the wedding. Sometimes, they know about the parents' choice and accept that choice. Sometimes, they are very shocked to learn about this after they grow up. This is the tradition for those families.

In India, some people fall in love first, like in the United States. These marriages are difficult in India because parents are often not happy. Parents do not usually trust this kind of marriage. They resist. Sometimes young lovers elope without their parents' permission. It takes a long time for the family to accept the couple.

Arranged marriage is very common in India. In this case, the families of the young people look for a good match. They look for someone from a good and respected family. They consider the personalities and interests of each person. The families agree first. Then the man and woman meet. They must both agree to marry. If they agree, the wedding can happen very quickly. Sometimes only one or two weeks pass between the meeting and the marriage. These are the most successful marriages in India. In my opinion, arranged marriage is the best way to make a happy marriage. The families know each other. They love their children. The children trust the parents' wisdom.

Wedding Celebrations in Serbia

OLIVERA PANIC

IN MY NATIVE COUNTY, SERBIA, engagements and weddings are special occasions. Some villagers still follow the old traditions. They celebrate for three days in a very traditional way. In big cities today, modern life changes the ways of weddings and engagements. People mix the modern lifestyle with old Serbian traditions.

First, the couple makes the decision to get married. The engagement begins with the man. He asks the woman's father for her hand in marriage. He also promises to take good care of her and provide a safe life and healthy children. Then the bride's family has an engagement party in their home. Both families attend the party. The best friends of the bride and groom also come to the party. At the beginning of the party, the man asks the woman to marry him. He gives her an engagement ring. The party starts after she says yes.

At the party, the groom's mom gives her future daughter-in-law a golden necklace and bracelet. The woman's family gives the couple bed sheets, towels, sleeping apparel, and blankets. Music, food, and drinks are special for this occasion, too. Old traditional Serbian songs are popular. New songs are popular, too. Each family chooses the food and drinks for the party. Some people mix different

European cuisine with traditional Serbian food. On every table are *rikija*, a strong type of brandy, and *pogaca*, home made bread. These symbolize wealth. The families talk about the wedding date, the place, and the wedding guests. The woman's family pays for the engagement and the man's family pays for the wedding.

On the wedding day in the morning, the groom has a pre-party at his house with family and close friends. They help him to get ready for his bride. Usually, at least one musician plays the accordion to create a party spirit. The guests drink and dance around the house and around the neighborhood. In the old tradition, the groom buys the bride from her brother or father. In older times, this was a very serious transaction. Today, people do it in the spirit of tradition and for good fun. The groom arrives at the bride's house with musicians and his family and friends. He negotiates the price for his future wife. The bride stays inside the house. Sometimes she even hides. Sometimes the groom's friends try to steal her. This negotiation is fun for the guests. When my good friend got married, her brother-in-law came through the window to steal her. It was very fun to see the faces of her brother and father. Traditionally, if the bride is stolen, the groom doesn't have to pay.

In Serbia, most people are Orthodox Christians. The couple always marries in church. The bride usually wears a white wedding dress and crown. She also holds a wax candle decorated with a red, pink, or white bow. The groom wears a tuxedo or fancy suit and a crown. He holds a candle as well. The priest talks to the couple and then asks them the most important question. He asks if they accept being husband and wife. They say yes. Then they exchange rings. They kiss each other. From that moment, they are husband and wife forever. This is one of the most beautiful moment of the wedding tradition. I still remember my cousin's wedding in the church. She looked like a princess, wearing a gorgeous pearl-color dress and a crown.

One very special part of the Serbian wedding is gypsy dancing and music. Usually in the middle of the wedding reception, a gypsy trumpet band arrives. Then the guests start a special dance. The band plays music for about an hour. During that time, everybody dances wildly. Some people dance on the tables and chairs. They sing loudly and have a lot of fun. After the gypsies leave the party, it is time for the wedding cake and champagne. Indeed, the cake is a sign for the bride and groom to leave. The couple leaves the wedding, but the guests are still having fun. They go on a trip or to some special place for their first night together.

It is very nice to mix old and new traditions for the perfect wedding.

The Polish Wedding Ceremony
MAGDALENA PTAK

MOST PEOPLE IN POLAND ARE Catholic. They usually get married in a Catholic church. However, the unique parts of the Polish wedding happen before the church ceremony and after the church ceremony.

On the wedding day, the groom and his parents arrive at the bride's home. They bring musicians with them. Soon friends and family of the bride and groom arrive. They offer blessings and good wishes to the couple. The blessing of the parents is especially important for the couple. If one of the parents already died, the wedding party will go the cemetery to ask for blessings from the deceased parent. Traditionally, the mother gives her blessing to the bride. After the blessings, everyone goes to the church.

Some traditions are part of modern marriage and connect to the past. For example, in the past, the bride's tears meant no tears during the marriage. If she did not cry at the wedding, she would cry throughout her marriage. Today, the tears are not necessary. In the past, everyone watched the couple at the end of the wedding ceremony. The actions of the couple reveal things about the marriage. Will the bride or the groom make the important decisions in the home? This shows from the way the couple leaves the altar. So they say...

After the ceremony, the guests greet the new couple outside the church. They stand in line to offer congratulations and best wishes. Then the guests throw small coins to the couple. The bride and groom must pick up the coins. This is a very old tradition. Sometimes people throw rice or grain. In villages, there is another tradition. Children put colorful ribbon on gates along the path from the church to the reception. They make the couple stop at each gate. The bride receives flowers and good wishes. The groom's friends give sweets to the children or wedding vodka to the adults. All the people of the village can participate a little in the celebration.

When the new couple arrives at the wedding house or reception place, the groom carries the bride over the threshold. The bride and groom enter together to symbolize a happy marriage. In an old custom, the parents greet the young couple at the door. The parents offer bread and salt to the couple. The bread symbolizes hunger. If you have bread, you will not be hungry. The salt reminds us of the difficulties of life. It will help the couple accept life's struggles. They also give wine to the couple. Wine will satisfy thirst and bring happiness and good health. Then the bride and groom sprinkle the salt on the bread. They taste the bread and drink the wine. Then they break the plate and the glass for good luck.

The wedding reception always has delicious food, alcohol, and dancing. The bride and groom dance the first dance. Then others can dance. Sometimes there is a money dance. The guests donate money to dance with the bride or groom. After each dance, the partner receives a drink and a piece of wedding cake. One more very important part of the Polish wedding is *oczepiny*. In this tradition, the bride's veil and the groom's tie can predict the next couple. They throw the veil and the tie. The single guests try to catch them and be the next bride or groom.

Polish weddings can be big or small. They can have only family. They can have a lot of family and friends. Some are formal, and some are informal. In each wedding the bride and groom receive blessings before going to church. They receive bread, salt, and wine. They predict the next bride and groom with *oczepiny*. Weddings are happy occasions.

Ethiopian Orthodox Marriage Ceremony

KONI TAMIRU

IN MY COUNTRY, ETHIOPIA, THERE are two kinds of marriages, arranged marriages and modern marriages. The arranged marriage is traditional in the villages. The parents arrange the marriage for their children. The bride and groom meet on their wedding day for the first time.

Modern marriages are very different. The bride and groom enjoy the wedding ceremony and the marriage. On the wedding day, the groom, his family, and his friends go to his bride's home to take her to the church. Usually the bride's family and friends hold the door closed to the groom. They try to keep him out. This is an amusing ritual for the beginning of a traditional marriage. After a while, he gets his bride. Her family and friends along with his family and friends sing and dance together. Then they go to the church. In the church, the bride and groom sit on special chairs facing the guests. Both wear a crown and a velvet robe with a big cross on it. These are from the priest at the church. The priest announces their wish to be married before God. The bride and groom make vows to each other. Then the church choir begins to sing traditional songs. The bride and groom walk through the guests. They join the choir and sing along with family and friends. Outside, the bride and groom stand next to their decorated horses. People take their picture as they walk to the reception. Their *Mize*, bridesmaids and best men, continue singing and dancing around the bride and groom.

Then, some of family members and friends go to the reception to welcome guests. Others follow the bride and groom. Some guests carry presents for the bride and groom. Most people carry long lighted candles. Inside the reception hall, the bridesmaids and the best men make an arch with the candles. The bride and groom walk underneath it as a sign of a bright future. The bride and groom stand and receive blessings from the priest. The priest prays for the guests and blesses the food. Next, they walk to their special table. The bridesmaids and best men serve food to the bride and groom. The food is made of different kinds of spices. These are very special for the wedding. For example, there is a special sauce called *doro watt*. It is made with chicken, onions, garlic, and spices. Other very special dishes include vegetables, beef sauces, and, of course, *injra* (bread). After the food is served, the priest asks the guests to rise. Young people take out brass rattles and line up facing each other. They sing hymns for the couple as they leave the reception. Then the groom takes his bride to his family's home.

CHAPTER FOUR

More Weddings

A Small, Simple Wedding
Vietnamese Engagement Ceremony
The Cambodian Wedding
My Two Weddings
Love and Marriage in Indonesia
Traditional or Modern?
Hope for a New Life
Chinese Weddings
A Simple Wedding

More Weddings

A Small, Simple Wedding

SARAH NIELSEN

*M*Y HUSBAND AND I HAD a small, simple wedding. We were both in our mid-thirties when we got married, so we didn't want a huge wedding. We both lived independently before getting married, so we didn't need a lot of presents to make a new household. We wanted our wedding day just for the two of us and for our families.

We wrote our own wedding vows, and my father married us. The ceremony was held in a beautiful park where we used to walk in the evenings when we were first dating. Surrounded by white flowers, our families stood around us in a circle. We read love poems to each other and exchanged our vows. After the ceremony, my brother and his wife hosted a small dinner with delicious food and a fluffy white cake.

It was the perfect day for us, small and simple.

Vietnamese Engagement Ceremony
NGOCHIEN VO

IN VIETNAM, THE ENGAGEMENT CEREMONY is festive and important. In some areas, especially in the countryside, the engagement is considered very important, even more important than the wedding. The parents of the bride and groom both make the arrangements for the celebration. This helps the two families know each other better.

Before the engagement day, each family chooses two representatives. They can be family members or friends. They are usually a happily married couple with a family of their own. The man is the one who actually does the representation. He requests the woman's hand in marriage on behalf of the fiancé's family. He helps with the exchange of gifts. He controls the flow of the ceremony. The families also negotiate the dowry and a date and time for the ceremony. Traditionally, the elder family members choose the date and time of the wedding. It is based on the dates and hours of birth of the bride and groom.

Several days prior to the engagement celebration, the groom's parents prepare gifts for the bride's family. These gifts include betel leaves, *areca* nuts, wine, tea, husband-wife cake, sticky rice, a whole roasted pig, and jewelry. These are placed in trays and wrapped in red plastic paper. The red paper will bring good luck. The bride's family prepares the ceremony.

On the engagement day, the groom's family carries the gifts to the bride's home. They greet the bride's family. Once everyone is inside, the groom's representative asks the bride's representative for her hand in marriage. The bride's representative graciously accepts the gifts. Together, the engaged couple prays in front of the family altar. There is a statue of the Buddha, a vase of flowers, and one candle holder on each side. Some families also have pictures of deceased ancestors. They ask their ancestors for approval. After praying, the groom places the engagement ring on the bride's finger.

Following the ring presentation, the representatives formally introduce all of the family members to each other. From this moment forward, the man and woman are officially members of their in-law's family. They should refer to their in-laws by their respective roles such as dad, mom, uncle, or aunt. The parents accept a new son or daughter into their own family. After the ceremony, the families celebrate the momentous occasion with a feast. The day after the engagement day, the engaged couple and their parents visit their neighbors, friends, and relatives.

Vietnamese culture and customs are unique in many ways. The engagement ceremony shows one of those unique customs.

The Cambodian Wedding
PHALLA PEL

A TRADITIONAL CAMBODIAN WEDDING IS A joyous occasion for the whole family. In Cambodia, a wedding can be very expensive or not so expensive. It depends upon the family situation. It can be elegant and grand, or it can be simple. Some things are the same in both cases. The families and friends come together to share the celebration in traditional ways.

The families of the bride and groom ask the Achar, a priest, to help them find a lucky day. Usually this depends upon the birthday of each person. On the day of the wedding, the bride waits at her parents' house. The groom brings his family and friends and lots of gifts. They walk in a procession to symbolize the journey of the bride and groom in finding each other. The people in the procession bring platters of gifts, roasted duck, roasted pig, roasted chicken, each one in a pair. The pairs of gifts symbolize the couple. They bring traditional fruits and desserts as well. Musicians play traditional music, and everyone can join in the songs.

The bride's family and friends wait at the front door to greet the procession. Then Buddhist monks will bless the new couple. Sometimes, three monks bless the couple. Sometimes five or seven offer blessings for the couple. The monks choose the blessings for each couple carefully. Every wedding has different blessings.

In the Khmer tradition in Cambodia, the couple prepares for the wedding with a cleansing ceremony. Singers and dancers surround the couple. The songs charm the couple with their beauty. In this ceremony, the bride and groom purify themselves to prepare for their new life. They hope for good fortune, beauty, and grace for their lives. The parents pretend to cut the hair of the bride and groom. This symbolizes throwing away misfortune. Then they sprinkle perfume on the couple.

Family ties are very important in Cambodian culture. In the wedding ceremony, the monk explains the importance of parents for each of us. We must give our parents gratitude and respect. They brought us into this world. In a special song, the words tell about the hardship of raising children. They remind the bride and groom of parental duty and fulfillment. The bride then holds an umbrella over her mother. This symbolizes the duty of married children to now protect their parents.

Next, married couples gather around the bride and groom. Three lit candles pass from person to person around the couple. The candles pass the couple seven times in this part of the ceremony. Each person passes a loving hand over the couple as a blessing. Only married couples participate in this part of the ceremony. They pass along the special blessing to preserve the marriage.

The last ritual before the reception is the knot tying ceremony. In this tradition, each guest ties a ribbon around the wrists of the bride and groom. These ribbons symbolize good wishes and blessings for the couple. The bride and groom wear these ribbons for three days after the wedding as good luck. Guests also wave palm leaves over the couple as a sign of good luck. This part of the ceremony is joyous. Everyone is ready for the music, food, friends, and family at the reception.

My Two Weddings
AMORNRAT GAULT

EVERY WOMAN DREAMS OF HER engagement and wedding, and so did I. I had double joy from the engagement and marriage. I got engaged and married two times, to the same groom. I'm Buddhist and my fiancé was Christian, so we had two weddings. I still remember very clearly the Christian wedding day on December 31, 2001 at Hale Koa Hotel in

Waikiki Beach. I also remember another happy day, the day of my Thai wedding with my family. My husband and I went back to Thailand and married again on April 18, 2002. We had a wonderful Thai ceremony. Both of our weddings were on New Year's Eve. Each wedding was the beginning of a new life together. In Thailand, April is the Thai New year.

My Thai wedding day was very special. We wanted a simple ceremony. My mother's friends came to the house very early in morning to cook and prepare for the wedding. My husband wore a white shirt and blue pants. I wore a beautiful pink Thai dress. Early in the morning, the monks came to bless us. Then we all ate breakfast together.

The food for the wedding day is *met khanoon*. *Met khanoon* is made in a brass wok from mung beans, eggs, coconut cream, and sugar. The taste is very sweet. *Met khanoon* means "seed of jackfruit." At a wedding, *met khanoon* symbolizes the dreams of the bride and groom. It also symbolized the support of the others. Another food is *khanom chan*. *Khanom chan* is made from rice flour, tapioca flour, and coconut milk, sugar, water, and various natural ingredients such as carrot and taro. Each piece is shaped into a rose, but *khanom chan* can be shaped into squares or any other shapes. This symbolizes the bride and groom moving forward in life and building a family.

The traditional wedding ceremony began in the afternoon at my parents' house. This is the most important part of the wedding ceremony. It is called Rod-Nam-Sang, water blessing. The water for this ceremony is in a conch shell. The name, Rod-Nam-Sang, comes from these words. *Rod* means soak. *Nam* is water. *Sang* is conch shell. Both the bride's family and the groom's family participate in this important event. My husband and I sat close together on the floor with our hands held in *wai* style. This is the way we pay respect to the lord Buddha. Flower chains connected our necks and hands. These chains made a crown of flowers, with jasmin and roses. Then my parents started to soak our hands in the blessing water and wished us good luck. Then, the members of my family, other relatives, and close friends did the same thing. Each one wished us good luck and happiness in our lives together. Our hearts are still full of those wonderful words.

On the same night, we had a wedding party in my parents' garden. There were many people there, family friends, neighbors, childhood friends, and relatives. We cooked lots of food. My aunts made cocktail drinks. I helped my mom and my aunts cook before the party. The party started with my sister. She talked and sang. Then she invited the guests to dance. Then my parents honored us with speeches. Both of them wished us happy lives together. They also gave us some tips for a happy marriage. For example, marriage is like chop sticks because you need both parts to get things done. Their advice was both amusing and helpful. I still remember their advice to be calm and cool in marriage.

Finally, we concluded the formal part of the ceremony. We enjoyed the night with eating, drinking, and dancing until midnight.

The two weddings were so special to me. I saw the joy on my parents' faces all day. I still remember their advice. Sometimes I look at the pictures in our wedding album and feel very happy. I married my husband twice, and each wedding was beautiful.

Love and Marriage in Indonesia

RATU F. BUCHANAN

THE REPUBLIC OF INDONESIA HAS many different cultures and languages. When I think about marriage in Indonesia, I must first imagine the family's culture. When I was married in Indonesia, we followed the traditions from Sumatra. This is what happened.

The parents of my fiancé sent an envoy to my parents house. They proposed for their son and asked if he could marry me, their daughter. My parents accepted their offer. Then my parents had the responsibility of organizing the wedding ceremony. This included the Siraman, or bathing ceremony, the Malam Ba'inah ceremony on the eve of the wedding, the Tunangan, or engagement ceremony, and the religious marriage celebration, the Ijab.

The first step of a wedding ceremony is a bathing ritual. It is called Siraman. In this ceremony, the bride and groom each bathe their body and their soul. This happens on the day before the wedding ceremony at each house. It could be in the bathroom, or it could be in the garden with some special preparation. Each family invites special guests to bathe the bride or groom. The traditional number of guests in seven. The water is prepared with garden flowers such as roses, jasmine, magnolia, and *cananga*. The order of each guest is also important. First the father and then the mother pour water over the bride or groom. Then the grandmother, grandfather, aunts and uncles, and respected elders do the same. I sat with both hands folded across my chest in a praying position. First we offered a prayer. Then each person poured water into my hands. I raised the water to my mouth three times. Then they each poured the water again on my head, face, ears, neck, hands and feet, each three times.

The next step is *Malam Ba'inah*. This ceremony takes place on the eve of the wedding ceremony. *Malam Ba'inah* means goddess. That evening, I became a beautiful goddess. According to ancient tradition, a goddess from heaven will visit the bride. I stayed in my beautifully decorated bedroom from 6 PM until midnight. An elderly woman stayed with me and gave me helpful advice. My soon-to-be husband came to my family's house. He could not see me, but he brought some gifts for me. This is the time for the parents to become in-laws.

The Ijab ceremony made our marriage legal. This ceremony can be in a mosque or in a large hall. The husband and wife make the vows to each other. They wear traditional clothes. I wore traditional makeup and a hair piece. It was covered with jasmine and jewels. This was a very important day in our lives.

Finally, the rituals finished, and we could go to the reception. At the reception, our family and friends honored us as the king and queen of the day. Some traditional Chinese dancers performed for us. Our families and friends offered us their blessings and good wishes. We all had a delicious meal and listened to traditional gamelan music. We smiled at each other, a happy married couple.

Traditional or Modern?

ANONYMOUS

MY BROTHER GOT MARRIED A few years ago. His wedding made me think a lot about traditional Japanese style engagements and weddings. In modern times, Japanese people have many options for engagement and marriage.

Some people are not interested in the traditional style. This worries me. The traditional style is hard to understand, but each generation should pass it to the next.

The traditional engagement in Japan is not a ceremony. It is a ritual. Japanese people usually imagine that a ceremony is lively and cheerful. A ritual is quiet and solemn. The engagement ritual is called *Yui-Nou* in Japanese. *Yui* means people linked to each other. *Nou* means people presenting something to each other. Originally, the ritual was in a private place, such as an old wooden house. This ritual is like a promise to get married. It is very formal and serious. Traditionally, a man never presents an engagement ring to a women. Instead, he presents Japanese traditional clothes to her. The clothes are called *ki-mono* in Japanese. The *ki-mono* is made of beautiful material. It is decorated with beautiful animals and colorful flowers.

Traditional marriage in Japan is also a ritual. The ritual is called *Ke-Kkon-Shiki* in Japanese. The wedding was usually held in a shrine in former times. These days, many people hold *Ke-Kkon-Shiki* in their houses. They wear formal clothes in the Japanese tradition. In this ritual, the bride and groom each sip alcohol three times. This is called *San-San-Ku-Do* in Japanese. Then, they pledge their marriage in front of God. Unlike Western marriage, the groom never presents a ring to the bride. This pledge is still not a legal marriage. The couple must register a form. Then the marriage is legal. The form is called *Kon-In-Todoke*.

In modern Japan, Western and Asian style weddings are very popular. For example, my brother presented an engagement ring to his girlfriend. Then, he held a formal engagement party with both families in his house. He did not present a *ki-mono* to her. It was different from *Yui-Nou*. Their wedding was different, too. It was held in a chapel.

The chapel was very beautiful. There were a lot of windows and sunshine in the chapel during the wedding. His friends and her friends, their coworkers, their bosses, and their families attended the ceremony. He presented a wedding ring to her. He wore a formal suit. She wore a beautiful pure white wedding dress. It was a Western style wedding.

Japanese couples have many choices for their engagement and wedding celebrations. Western style weddings are popular. However, I think Japanese people should not lose the original Japanese styles. Japanese traditional rituals are still an important part of Japanese culture.

Hope for a New Life
HYE-IN CHUNG

MY WEDDING DAY SO MANY years ago was the most remarkable event of my life. It changed my life completely. It was also a very special event for everyone in our families. Our marriage promise to each other included a promise to our families. I always enjoy the memories of my wedding day.

The first step in preparing for a wedding was a dinner with our parents. We met in a restaurant to have dinner and discuss the details of our wedding plans. We planned the date and the place. In Korea, the families give gifts to each other. The gifts depend upon the family traditions and the family income. The gifts might include Korean clothing, Hon-Bok. They might also include bedding and furniture. The parents help the new couple establish their first home.

On the day before the wedding ceremony, my husband visited my house with his friends. He gave my parents a box, called *ham*. This box is a gift from the groom's parents. It includes a wedding gift for the bride, red clothes, blue clothes, and a letter to the bride's parents. This letter thanks the parents for allowing the marriage. I still have the gifts and the letter from my husband's parents.

Modern couples in Korea can decide about the style for their own wedding. Weddings can be in a church or a wedding hall. It depends upon the family and the family's religion. My husband and I wanted a Catholic wedding. The ceremony began with a hymn. Then the priest performed our marriage rites. We promised to love each other forever. That was the most unforgettable moment of my life.

My husband and I also wanted to include *pae-baek*. This is a traditional Korean ceremony. In this ceremony the bride greets the parents and relatives of the groom's family after the wedding ceremony. The bride bows to each member of the family. My husband has a big family, so I made a lot of deep bows to his family.

After our honeymoon, my husband and I spent one night with his parents and one night with my parents. We had a small party at each house. Our parents wished us happiness in our lives. Now when I go to a wedding, I always think about my own wedding with great happiness. I remember the moment of my heart throbbing with hope for the future.

Chinese Weddings

XILEI YAN

WEDDINGS FOR CHINESE PEOPLE ARE a gate to another life. The modern style of celebrating this important event is very different from traditional Chinese wedding celebrations. People can choose the traditional style or the modern style.

On the day of a traditional wedding, both the bride's house and the groom's house are decorated in red. The groom's family will send a procession of servants, musicians, and a carriage to the bride's house. They will bring her back to his house. The bride always wears a red gown. Also, a red silk cloth will cover her face. In a traditional Chinese wedding, only the groom can see the bride's face. At the bride's house, the groom will carry the bride on his back to the carriage. According to custom, the bride's feet cannot touch the ground until she arrives at the groom's house. The wedding is at the groom's house, and all the relatives and friends are witnesses.

First, the bride and the groom will worship heaven and earth. Then they pray to the groom's ancestors. Finally, they bow to each other. After that, the new couple serves tea to all of their respected elders. They receive a red package with some money from each one. Then, the bride goes into the bridal room, and the groom's family has a feast. After the dinner, the groom goes to the bridal room. He will take off the red cloth from the bride's face. They have a drink together and eat some candies and peanuts. These symbolize a long life and lots of children.

Nowadays, the modern Chinese wedding is a little bit different from the traditional one. On the wedding day early in the morning, the groom and his family will decorate the car and drive to the bride's house. At the door, the bridesmaid will prepare a lot of difficult questions, such as "Why should I open the door?" The groom has to answer all the questions. This proves his ability to take care of the bride. It is also fun. Sometimes the groom sings out his love for the bride. The groom also prepares some money for the bridesmaids. He has to pay them for entrance into the house. Finally, he enters and meets the bride. She wears a white dress in modern times. The new couple serves tea to the elders in the bride's family. Then they go to the wedding feast in a restaurant.

The wedding feast is the parents' gift to their relatives. During the feast, the guests always sit at round tables. The guests enjoy visiting and talking about the happy couple. Before the feast, the bride changes into a red gown, a traditional color for good luck. Then the new couple walks from table to table. They toast the guests and thank them for coming. In return, the guests toast the bride and the groom. At the end of the feast, the new couple stands at the door to thank the guests. They wish them well as they leave.

Both the traditional Chinese wedding and modern Chinese wedding are still popular today in China. For Chinese people, the wedding ceremony is the most important event in their lives.

A Simple Wedding
MARIA A. VARGAS

HE LOVES ME; HE LOVES me not. He loves me; he loves me not. He loves me; he loves me not. True love sometimes begins with a flower and a hope. Sometimes it includes marriage. In Colombia, a happy marriage starts with some important traditions.

After the lovers decide to get married, the man must speak to the parents of the woman. This makes men very nervous. My brother-in-law told us about his nightmare before he talked to our parents. He dreamed about snakes eating his brain. He laughs about it now, but not then. The young man must invite the parents of his girlfriend to an elegant dinner. They spend the evening talking about nothing special. After dessert, the young man then tells the parents of his love for their daughter. He asks about marriage, the father says yes, and finally they have wine and rejoice. The soon-to-be-bride waits at home, hoping for a happy answer.

Preparing for the wedding takes several months. The bride and her mother make all of the arrangements. They select the reception hall, the food, the flowers, the decorations, and the music for the reception. They also make the guest list. Of course, they also select the perfect wedding gown. The months before the wedding are very busy for the bride and her family.

One lovely tradition in Colombia is the *cerenata*. On the night before the wedding, the groom goes to the bride's house with a group of musicians. They serenade at the soon-to-be bride's window. They sing love songs, and the groom sends flowers to his love. This is a very romantic moment in the wedding tradition.

The wedding day brings great joy to everyone. The bride looks beautiful, and the groom looks handsome. After the long preparations, they are both happy to finally be husband and wife. After the ceremony, everyone goes to the reception for dinner and dancing. This is the beginning of a long and happy life.

Having a Baby

 # Having a Baby

The Birth of My Twins

GABRIELA ANTEZANA

OUR FAMILIES CELEBRATED THE ARRIVAL of a new baby in some special ways in Bolivia. It is customary for the families of the mother and father to go to the doctor's office with the parents. They want to be there to learn if the baby is a boy or a girl. My family did that for me and my husband, too. At the end of five months of pregnancy, we all went to the doctor's office together. The doctor was a little worried about my size. My stomach was very, very big. She decided to do a special test to make sure my baby was safe. We were excited about seeing a life-like image on a special machine. The doctor put gel on my stomach for the ultrasound. First we could see the baby's face, and hands, and feet. The doctor said, "It's a girl." Then she said, "It's a boy." We all laughed, but the doctor said, "You have twins!" Then we saw images of our twins. It was a big surprise for our entire family. It was also a very happy moment. I cried. Our parents cried. These were all tears of joy. That night, we celebrated with a special dinner. My husband and family drank wine, and I drank water. We were all very happy.

A few weeks before the birth, my husband's family hosted a party for me and our babies. No men are invited to this party. It was a baby shower. My mother-in-law decorated the house with flowers and lots of pink and blue baby decorations. She made *empanadas* with cheese, cookies, and a big cake. The cake had decorations of two babies on top. All of the women in my family and in my husband's family were there. Many of my friends came, too. We ate lunch and then had tea. Friends from college and from my job brought gifts for our babies. One gift was handmade clothes for each baby. My friend's mother designed and made these baby clothes, one for a girl and one for a boy. I opened the gifts and felt so happy. My babies already had so many generous friends.

Finally the babies came. Everyone in our families came to the hospital to see them. Twins are very unusual in Bolivia. Everyone wanted to see them. They sent flowers and cards. Friends sent hats, clothes, pampers, wipes, blankets, towels, and everything the babies needed.

My heart was overflowing with love. I never imagined how much love was in me. Now I am very happy to be the mother of two wonderful children.

Giving Birth
ANONYMOUS

My EXPERIENCE WITH HAVING A baby is very typical of Chinese birth tradition. My baby was due on April 12, 1991. I lived in Nanjing, and my friends gave me advice about what to do. About two weeks before the birth, they told me to cut my hair very short. We cannot wash our hair for one month after the baby comes. Wet hair can cause headaches later. They also had other advice. Do not take a shower or bath for one month. Do not wear slippers. Slippers can cause heel pain. I should wear warm shoes only. A new mother should not read. No reading for one month. Reading can cause eye problems. Finally, a new mother should not do any housework.

My husband hired a young maid to help me for one month. The maid did not have experience. I did many things by myself. I did try to follow the traditions. These traditions are important. Women know about their bodies. They teach their friends to take good care of their bodies. It takes at least one month for our body to return to normal after a baby.

Modern women do not follow these traditions very much. They think a frequent shower or bath is always important. Most people are in good health now, so these old traditions are not so important.

Chinese Celebrations

YAN YANG

IN CHINESE CULTURE, FOUR IMPORTANT celebrations welcome the new baby. Several days after the birth, we announce the birth to the village. The father goes to each home with a special gift. The family prepares red dyed eggs for a boy or sticky rice cake for a girl. These symbolize peace and good luck. The father gives them to their neighbor and friends. This custom is very old in China. Eggs and rice are precious and very nutritious. A newborn brings the family peace and good luck. We share the good luck and our joy with our relatives, friends, and neighbors.

After one month, most families have a party. They invite relatives and important friends. We serve our guests the best food and wine. Each guest prepares some lucky money or gold for the baby. They put the gifts in a vivid red envelope or box. During the party, we have a special ceremony. We shave the baby's hair. Later we make a writing brush with the hair. We do this for two reasons. The baby's hair will grow thicker, and the parents can give the special writing brush to the child in later years.

One hundred days after the birth, we have another tradition. One hundred is a lucky number. It represents long life and fulfillment. This is a day to record the baby's development. The parents take a picture, or they go to a studio for a portrait. This portrait is another treasure for the child in later years.

On the first birthday, we have another traditional activity. This is a big celebration for family and friends. It is important for the baby, too. At this celebration, the baby will pick a career. The baby will choose one item among twelve items. Each item symbolizes a career or a quality.

When the baby picks one, it predicts the future. This is not scientific, but it is amusing. Each item is very special and represents something about life. These are an abacus, a book, a coin, a pen, a seal, meat, a sword, a globe, a ruler, celery, an orange, and a green onion. My own baby had fun at this celebration. She crawled on the floor and played with almost everything. She finally chose a ruler. This was a soft tape measure for sewing. She wrapped it all around herself in delight. We have pictures of this as a treasure for her book of memories of her childhood. It offers her our best wishes for her future.

We are first generation immigrants to the United States. We don't have relatives here. It is difficult to enjoy most of the traditional celebrations. We do have friends and neighbors. They celebrated with us like a family. Our first year of parenting was a memorable and valuable experience.

In Sikh Culture

KAJAL

THE BIRTH OF A CHILD in a family is an occasion of joy and happiness for the family. Birth is the first stage of life. In the Sikh religion the pregnant lady wears a special kind of bracelet on her arm. It is a religious bracelet. The pregnant woman's mother gives her this bracelet. It is made of special beads. This bracelet has power to protect the mother and the baby from bad spirits. Also a pregnant woman should not go to any funerals. A funeral can be dangerous for the mother and the baby.

For the first baby, the pregnant woman lives with her mother for the last two months of pregnancy. She gives birth to the first baby at her mother's house. She must stay in a warm place. She cannot take a shower for ten days after the birth. For the second baby and all other babies, the mother does not stay with her mother.

After the birth, we have a special ceremony to choose a name for the baby. The name gives a baby unique identity. The name is sacred. Before the ceremony the mother and baby bathe. They must be clean and pure. The new parents and the baby go to the Gurdwara, a Sikh temple. Relatives and friends go to this special religious place. Everyone prays and asks for blessing for good health and a long life. They pray for a Sikh way of life. Then they open the Guru Granth Sahib, our holy book, to any page. This is not planned. The first letter of the first word on the page becomes the first letter of the baby's name. Every girl is also *Kaur*, meaning princess. Every boy is always *Singh*, meaning lion. This naming ceremony ends with a reception. Everyone has sweets to celebrate the joyous occasion.

Korean's Traditional Culture

HAYEON KIM

I HAVE TWO CHILDREN. THE FIRST child, my daughter, was born in Korea. My son was born in the USA. Each birth was very different. In my country, South Korea, I did not have a special celebration like a baby shower. During pregnancy, Tae Gyo, I influenced my unborn baby. This is important to every Korean pregnant women and unborn baby. The mother's feelings influence the baby's future and the baby's appearance. If the mother looks upon beautiful people, the baby will resemble those people. If she looks upon someone with hate, the baby will resemble that person. Also, the pregnant woman must eat good food, use good words, and listen to good sounds. This will be good for the baby's personality and behavior. Our ancestors believed these things. Now we still believe these things. I did these things when I was pregnant.

In Korea, special food is very important for pregnancy and for a new mother. After the birth of my daughter, I ate seaweed soup. It is called *meeyeokgook*. I also drank pumpkin tea. My mom gave me good advice. *Meeyeokgook* purifies the blood, and pumpkin tea helps with weight loss. I ate warm food and touched warm water. I did not lift heavy things for three weeks after the birth. I could not take a shower for seven days. In Korea, these are very common ideas from older times. Our ancestors taught us these important things to keep us in good health. A woman must follow these traditions. If not, she will have many body pains at forty years old. Many women talk about the aches starting at forty years old.

Keeping the rules after a baby's birth are traditional Korean culture. These rules were helpful for me and my children. I will teach my daughter about these rules in the future.

Birth Traditions in Russia

ANONYMOUS

$\mathcal{R}$USSIA HAS A VERY LONG history, more than eight hundred years. There are many old and strong traditions in Russia. Some traditions about the birth of a new baby seem like superstitions, but not to Russians. For us these are very important cultural and family traditions.

In Russia a pregnant woman doesn't tell everyone immediately. Even relatives find out from seeing a woman's growing belly. No one touches her belly. No one has a baby shower. It is bad luck to give a gift for the baby before the birth. In Russia, we never celebrate a birthday before the actual day. This is especially important for a young child. The early celebration can cut the number of days to live. No one wants a short life. This is the reason for no baby shower. We never give a gift before the birthday.

In Russia, women usually deliver their babies in a special hospital. A woman goes to the hospital at the very late stage of pregnancy. Some wait until signs of labor. Women stay after delivery for ten days. This hospital is only for women and doctors. No one attends the birth. After the delivery, the doctors monitor the mother and the baby. Husbands can see their babies through a hospital window for the first few days. In my hometown, a new father hangs a sign outside the window. It says welcome to the new baby and thank you to the mother.

Russia also has traditions about the new baby coming home from the hospital. We put all of our valuable things on the bed. These could be expensive fur coats, gold and platinum jewelry, diamond jewelry, and other luxury items, even money. Then we put the baby on the bed. In this way, we wish our baby a better financial future.

For thirty days after the birth, only the parents can see the baby. We believe that a new baby does not yet have a guardian angel. The parents must protect the baby from a bad person or an evil look. They protect the baby's soul. After that, all the relatives and friends can meet the new baby.

In the United States, these traditions are unusual. It can be difficult to live here and keep our cultural traditions. My husband's family does not always understand my thinking. Sometimes I have to give up Russian traditions and accept a new lifestyle. These traditions will always be a part of me.

Giving Birth in Taiwan

JIAYU LIU

WOMEN MUST BE VERY CAREFUL during pregnancy. In Taiwan, women have many taboos during pregnancy. These are superstitions, and some women do not believe them today. Many women do follow these traditions. They are very interesting. First, a pregnant woman cannot hold scissors in the bedroom. The baby could be born with a defect. The pregnant woman cannot move furniture in the house, especially the bed. Actually, no one should move furniture in the house during this time. The baby could have a problem finding directions later in life. Everything in the pregnant woman's life can influence the baby. My mother saw a fire in the neighborhood. My sister has a red mark above her eye because my mother was pregnant at the time. Everyone must be very careful during pregnancy.

After the baby arrives, the mother should not take a shower or wash her hair for one month. These ideas are from older times. The water was not always clean then. Many people could get infections.

Another tradition from older times is the first birthday celebration. We put several things in a basket. These are money, an abacus, a writing brush, and some toys. The baby chooses something from the basket. This will tell the future. The abacus shows good mathematics skills. Money means wealth. The writing brush means knowledge and skill with language. In ancient times, this was serious. Now it is a fun game.

Born in Ukraine
ANONYMOUS

I WAS BORN IN UKRAINE IN 1976. At that time, women delivered babies in a special hospital. Only medical doctors and nurses could be in that hospital with the new mothers and babies. I was five days old when my father first held me. He took me home on that day. Today, the father and other close relatives can enter the hospital and stay in the delivery room.

At home, the baby was with only the mother and father. They protected the baby at home for forty days. In some old superstitions, the baby's soul was not yet with the body. The parents must protect the baby from bad luck or bad spirits. Today, we protect the baby from germs and disease.

After those forty days, the parents can take the baby to the church. In the church ceremony, the parents ask for God's protection for the baby. They also give the baby a name. Before the ceremony, the mother cannot eat meat for one week. She prays at home every day. She also goes to church to confess her sins. The pastor then asks her to say special prayers. Then they select a date for the church ceremony. The parents ask two special people to be the godmother and godfather. The godparents, relatives, and friends wear formal clothes to the ceremony. The church is decorated with beautiful flowers. During the ceremony, the priest puts a cross on a chain. He puts this around the baby's neck. The godfather holds the baby and says special prayers. The priest pours water on the baby's head. This ceremony welcomes the baby into the church and protects the baby from bad luck. We also select the baby's name from a special book. The names come from the past and bring good characteristics to the baby.

In Ukraine, we do not have baby showers. We do not give the baby any gifts before the birth. This brings bad luck to the baby. After forty days, the parents can invite friends and family to meet the baby. They have a party. Guests bring gifts for the baby. Some people bring clothes or baby supplies. Some give family treasures, something from a grandmother or grandfather. They tell the story of these things at the party.

Traditions in Ukraine are changing quickly in modern times. The traditions from my childhood are already different from today. Now I am in the USA, and my own children will have different traditions.

A New Life Starts
LY LE

In my country, vietnam, our cultural traditions continue with each new generation. We celebrate and greet each new life joyfully, happily, and proudly. The celebration at birth brings the baby good luck and prepares the baby for a good life.

I have two brothers and two sisters, and we all lived together. My older sister was the first member in my family to get pregnant. We were all excited about that. Each member of my family prepared something special for the baby. My mom and I made clothes. My brothers bought a lot of toys. My sister and her husband painted the room. The baby was always the topic of conversation. I could see the happiness on every face in my family. Soon I noticed the happiness in our neighbors. They too felt excited about the baby coming. Our neighbors asked about the baby. They also predicted the baby's gender. They looked at my sister's belly. One neighbor predicted a boy baby. The pointed shape of my sister's belly indicated a boy. Our neighbor was correct. My sister had a boy.

In Vietnam, we have a baby shower one month after the birth. We invited some close friends, relatives, and neighbors to join with us. They brought many gifts for my nephew. They gave him money, toys, clothes, and food as well. My family prepared a dinner for our guests.

Our family's religion is Buddhism. We follow Buddhist traditions for having a baby. First, we decorate our ancestor's altar. Each home has a special altar for ancestors. It has an image of Buddha. It also has pictures of our ancestors. This special altar reminds us every day of our religion and of our ancestors. On the altar, we have a small jar of incense.

We burn incense there every day. We also clean up and decorate the altar for special occasions. My sister's baby was a very special occasion.

We have another celebration for the baby. On this day, the baby will tell his own future. First my sister put many things on the floor. She put a pencil, a book, a ruler, a stethoscope, and a tennis racket. Then my sister put her baby on the floor. Everybody watched to see the baby grab something. In my culture, we believe that a baby predicts his future with his choice on that day. Will he be a teacher, a writer, a doctor? My nephew chose the tennis racket. He will be a tennis player in the future. His choice made sense to my family. His daddy is a tennis coach. Perhaps the tradition is mostly for fun, but we keep the tradition from generation to generation. This is how we greet the new baby.

Our family prepared a baby shower for his little sister five years later. My family does not live together now. My parents and I immigrated to the United States. We were still excited about the baby. We were curious about her prediction for her future. We could not watch, but we felt joyful and happy from far away.

CHAPTER SIX

Naming Traditions

Naming Traditions

Naming Traditions in Japan
MAKI KOGA

*O*UR PARENTS CHOOSE OUR NAMES. The names are their choice and reflect their taste. My parents took great care in choosing my name. The traits associated with my first name affected my personality. This was my parents' intention. Japanese people do not use a middle name. We have only a first name and a last name. Parents try to balance these two names.

Most Japanese names are written in Kanji, Chinese characters. These Chinese characters have Chinese meaning and Japanese pronunciation. Each character has many strokes or lines. Simple words have two or three strokes. Complex words have seven or more strokes. My name is Maki. It has 15 strokes. There are two Kanji characters. Three strokes for Ma and 12 strokes for Ki. My grandmother chose this name for me. It was her best friend's name. In Kanji, it means much happiness. Maki is a common name in Japan. However, my parents chose a very rare Kanji for my name. As a matter of fact, I have never met someone with the same name in Kanji. My grandmother and my parents loved not only the meaning but also the pronunciation of Maki. First, my parents chose my name. Then they asked the fortune teller for approval. The fortune teller makes predictions about the future from the number of stroke counts in the Kanji name. After that, the name is final. This custom is still popular in Japan, but it is changing now. It is popular to use special books for advice on names. Japanese female names often end with –ko. Names like Akiko, Keiko, Masako, and Yoko are very popular. The meaning of -ko in Kanji is a child. At the end of a name, it is always a female's name. Historically, only daughters of the Imperial family had names ending in –ko. Then it became popular for many families. Beginning in 1980, Japanese parents changed the style. Now many girls' names do not have –ko. In my elementary school, most of the girls had names ending in -ko. I always wanted to have a name ending with –ko. I wanted to be like them. I blamed my parents then.

Over the last few decades, popular boy names also changed in Japan. Many parents used to name their son with a number in Kanji. They combined the number with another Chinese character. For example, *ichi* was a popular number. It means one. Ichiro means the first in Kanji. Another popular name is Jiro. It means two or second in Kanji. This shows the boy's place in the family. Families are smaller now. It is not necessary to have numbers in names now.

I believe a name gives a person a special identity. I appreciate my parents for giving me my name.

Japanese Names

MASAYA TSUBAKIYAMA

IN JAPAN, CHILDREN RECEIVE TWO names. One is a family name. The family name is passed down from generation to generation by the man. The other name is the first name. The first name describes the hope of the parents. The family name in Japan originates from the thing, the place, or the custom of ancestors. For example, my family name is Tsubakiyama. My ancestors lived near the mountains. There were many flowers around the mountain. Tsubaki means camellia in English. This is a beautiful flower. Yama means mountain in English. My ancestor's family name is Tsubakiyama. They loved the beautiful sight of the flowers and the mountain.

Japanese first names describe the wishes and hopes of their parents for the new baby. Parents and grandparents hope the new baby will grow up with the personal qualities of their name. For example, Makoto means sincerity in English. Akiko means bright or cheerful in English. Sakura means cherry in English. Sakura describes luxury and generosity.

Japanese first names seem very different from first names in western countries. We like to use names from nature or from our ideas of important personal qualities.

Difficult Decision in China

JESSICA ZHU

A CHINESE NAME USUALLY HAS THREE parts, first name, middle name, and family name. In traditional Chinese customs, only a boy received the family name. Only male children were considered family members. A female child will become a member of her husband's family. She did not receive the family name. Since 1979 in China, each family has only one child. This one-child policy caused some changes for naming traditions. The new baby will be the only child or grandchild in each family. Grandparents from the mom's side and grandparents from the dad's side want to choose a name. The parents also want to choose the name for their baby. This situation can cause an argument. Each set of parents has different ideas.

For grandparents from the mom's side, the baby's name creates a family bond. This bond is very important. In Chinese culture, the children care for their elderly parents and grandparents. Men must care for their parents or grandparents as family members. A woman cares for her husband's family first. Then she cares for her own parents or grandparents. Grandparents and parents of female children lose a daughter or granddaughter with her marriage. This can be very sad for them. They want to pick a name to build a relationship with the female child. This can be a first name or a middle name. The name helps the grandchild remember them. For example, perhaps the grandpa's name is Jun pei Bei. The baby's name could be Jun plus another name.

The grandparents from the dad's side are responsible for the family name. Grandparents from the dad's side follow Chinese tradition. They are in charge of naming the new baby. The grandchild receives a name from the father's side. Before the one-child policy, every grandchild in one generation received the same middle name. The oldest grandfather picked the middle name. The new baby's grandparents from the father's side choose the first name. They choose a name with special meaning. The name could mean luck, health, wealth, or long life. For example, a boy's name could be Bai He. It means long life and perfect poise.

For the mother and father the name is also very important. With a one-child policy, they have only one baby to name. The baby's name is very important now. They want the grandparents to be happy with the names. Some parents pick a name related to both families. For example, the boy's name Suo Chen combines two family names. Suo is from the father's side. Chen is from the mom's family.

The one-child policy affects family culture. The name for a new baby is a difficult choice for parents and grandparents now.

Naming in Ukraine
ANONYMOUS

In ancient times, in ukraine, a priest always participated in naming a baby. No one chose a name without a participating priest. In modern times, people have more choices. Still, religion has a big influence in choosing a name in Ukraine. Forty percent of Ukrainians belong to Orthodox Christianity. They choose a baby's first name from the saint day. For example, a baby born on December nineteenth will be named Nicolai. Nicolai is one of the most famous saints in Orthodox Christianity. Sometimes parents have a favorite saint. They give this name to the baby. They hope the child will have the same qualities as the saint. The baby's saint will be an angel-protector for the baby during his or her life.

Some parents choose a name to honor a member of a family. For example, a mother might name her daughter the same name as her mother. She might give her son the name of her father. The grandmother or grandfather will watch over the child all through his or her life. Even after the grandparents die, they continue to protect the child. Not everyone likes this custom. They worry about the child having some bad qualities of the deceased grandparents.

Many people in Ukraine do not have any tradition for choosing a name for a baby. They search in books to learn the meaning of each name. Some people name their newborns for a flower, like Rose or Lily. Some like the sound of a name. My older sister chose my name. She liked it and my mother agreed.

Now, many people like to take names of famous people, especially their favorite actors. Some children have traditional names, such as Nicolai, Sergei, Olga, or Elena. Others have famous names, like Angelina, Tom, or Arnold.

Ukrainian parents make their own choices for naming their babies.

Our Naming Traditions
NANA AFUA SERWAH

I AM FROM THE ASHANTI KOTOKO tribe in the heart of Ghana. Ashanti Kotoko is one of the fifty-two tribes in Ghana. Each tribe has its own way of naming their babies.

The first name is the soul name of the baby. The day of birth determines the soul name. Males and females have different soul names. For example, a boy baby born on Sunday is named Akwasi. A female will be Akosua. A Monday male is Kojo, and the female is Adowa. The soul name carries your destiny. I was born on Friday. My name is Afua. A male child is named Kofi. Every child born on Friday is humble and quiet. We don't talk much. We are respectful, and we have dignity.

We also have a middle name. Our parents name us after our godparents. Our last name is from our family. This is a *den pa*. In my tribe everybody has at least three names, a soul name, a middle name, and a last name. I have five names. I was named after a queen mother of the Ashanti tribe. We do not call the queens by their names. We give them titles like Nana or Maame. They mean mother. My first name is Nana. My soul name is Afua. My middle name is Kobi. My last name is Serwah. I also have a royal name, Ampem.

The actual naming ceremony is eight days after the birth. It affects the spirit of our soul. The baby's father chooses an elder from his family to perform the naming ceremony. Sometimes the father can name the baby after himself. Sometimes the father honors a friend by giving the baby his name. Then the babies will receive the father's family name, the *den pa*. This is the baby's surname.

The naming ceremony begins at six o'clock in the morning and ends at six o'clock in the evening. In the morning, both families arrive at the father's house. They pour liberations to invoke our ancestors. The elder says the soul name and the surname of the baby aloud for the first time. At the ceremony there are two cups. One cup contains water, and one contains alcohol. The elder holds the baby and dips one finger in the water. Then he puts it on the baby's tongue. He says, "This is water." He repeats this three times to the baby. The same procedure is repeated, but with alcohol. It symbolizes a world full of mysteries. The family shares the remaining water and alcohol among themselves.

The ceremony is also a time for gifts. The first gift is always from the person the baby is named for. He or she will put a ring on the baby's finger and put money in his or her hand. Then everybody brings their gifts to the baby. At the ceremony, we have African drums. We dance to the music. The dance is called Adowa. Everyone dances in a circle around the baby. We also eat African food. We serve *banku* and okra stew, *fufu* and soup, rice balls and peanut soup. People eat, drink, and dance until sunset.

Names in Mexico
JOSE TORRES

CHOOSING THE RIGHT NAME FOR a new baby is not easy. The names are one of many things that give us a special and unique identity. Parents always want a beautiful and unique name. Sometimes, parents choose names before the birth. Sometimes they do not. Sometimes, parents and relatives argue about the name of the baby. In my country, México, we have many traditions for choosing names for children. Some people choose the father's name. Some search for the name according to a special birth calendar. Some people look in books with names and name meanings.

In some families, the first born son receives the father's name. The first born daughter receives the mother's name. This is a tradition in Mexico. It is a tradition in my family, too. For example, my father's name is Jose, and my grandfather's name was Jose. They named me Jose. I will probably name my first son Jose. I have many friends with their father's first name. My friend Eduardo has his father's name. It is also his grandfather's name. Perhaps it will be the name of his first son.

Some parents search a church calendar on the day the baby is born. They choose a name from the saint name or special meaning for that day. For example, my best friend, Ramona, was born on August Thirty-first. The calendar shows the name Ramon for a boy and Ramona for a girl. These are both very nice names. Sometimes the name is not so beautiful, but the meaning is beautiful. My friend, Inocencia, was born on December Twenty-eighth. In Mexico, this is the day of the innocents. So, her parents called her Inocencia. She never liked her name. My cousin, Calixto, also does not like his name. He was born on October Fourteenth, and the calendar shows that name. These friends do not like the tradition of using the church calendar.

In another tradition, parents pick a name from a book. The book has the meaning of hundreds of names. The parents look for a beautiful name with an important meaning. Sometimes they want a unique or unusual name. For example, my friend, Megan, has a special name. Her name means strong and capable. Her name shows her real identity. My sister's friend is Pedro. His name means love and friendship. I think he really is a very loving good friend. My niece's name is Monica. Her mother wanted a beautiful name with a strong meaning. Monica means advisor. She really is a person with good advice for others.

A name is part of our personality. Our names are an important part of us. Parents should always choose very carefully.

Name Traditions

HUGO VERA

I ASKED MY CLASSMATES ABOUT THEIR names. Almost half of them did not know the meaning of their names. They did not know the reason for their names. This was a surprise to me. I was born in a big traditional Mexican family. There are six sons and four daughters. We lived in a small city with Catholic influence. The Catholic religion has a strong influence. It also influences the name for a baby. In the past, this was always true. Now that tradition is changing.

The parents found the baby's name on a special calendar. Almost every family in the country followed this tradition. They used it until the middle of the last century. It is a very old tradition. It probably comes from the Spanish. Spain was a Catholic country. It brought religious traditions to Mexico. It also brought the saint calendar. The religious calendar comes with the name of a saint below the date. A baby receives the name for the day of birth. For example, my brother, Martin, was born on November Eleventh. On this day, the name below the number is Saint Martin. My mom was born on November Twenty-seventh. The name on that day is Saint Antonieta. Her name is Antonia. The parents could change the name slightly. Many of my friends got their names in this tradition.

There are two very special days in Mexico. December Twenty-fifth is the birthday of Jesus. A boy born on this day receives the name Jesus. In Mexican culture, these boys are very special. They have a special blessing. December Twelfth is the feast of Our Lady of Guadalupe. This is a very important religious holiday in Mexico. Girls born on this day are named Maria Guadalupe. These two days are the most important days for the people in Mexico. Many women in Mexico have Maria as a first name. This name is in honor of the mother of Jesus.

Not every child in my family got a name from the calendar. I got my name from a famous Mexican soccer player. His name is Hugo Sanchez, so my name is Hugo. I like the tradition of naming from the past. It was exiting and very important. Many traditions are different now.

My Family Names

MARILYN MARQUIS

IN THE UNITED STATES, THERE are no national traditions or customs for naming children. Some of our family customs come from our ancestors in countries around the world. We give a new baby the father's surname, most of the time. Married women take their husband's last name, most of the time. In modern times, families make choices according to their own ideas. Following tradition is a personal decision. My family has some interesting naming traditions.

My mother's family is Italian Catholic. Everyone must have a saint name. Her older sisters were studying Russian history before her birth. They were interested in Princess Olga. They begged their mother to name the new baby Olga. One Sunday during her pregnancy, my grandmother was at mass. The priest told the congregation to name one child Michael. Saint Michael was the protector of God. My mother became Olga Michalina, Russian princess and protector of God.

My parents took great care with naming their children. Each name is special. My older brother has our father's name. Our father also has his father's name, Donald Lawrence Marquis. Now four generations of first born son's have the same name. My sister's name is Pamela Ann Marquis. Her initials spell her nickname, Pam. My name is Marilyn Marie Marquis. My initials are MMM, (delicious). My younger brother is Gregory Edward Marquis. He is a gem, something of great value.

My daughters both have the same initials for their first names and middle names, Michelle Monique, and Madeline Marie. They are each named after someone special. Their father was Michael. Michelle has a form of his name. Madeline has the name of my mother's best friend. I loved her very much, too. I honored her, and I hoped my own daughter would have some of her qualities.

My daughter, Michelle, married Joe. In his family, the first born son has the grandfather's name. All first born sons in his family are Joe or Harry. My daughter accepted Joe's offer of marriage only after she agreed to name her son Harry. Her daughter is Margaret Maura and her son is Harry. Each one has a special feeling from sharing their names with other generations in the family.

In my family, our names connect us to each other and our larger culture in many different ways. We each enjoy having a special story with our names.

CHAPTER SEVEN

Holidays

Chinese Moon Festival

Chuseok

El Dia de Los Muertos

A Day for the Living and the Dead

The Zapopan's Virgin

Virgin of Guadalupe

Christmas With My Family

Christmas, New Traditions

Three Kings' Day

A Special Family Day

Saint John the Baptist, June 24

Inti Raymi

After Ramadan

Chaharshanbesuri

Holidays

Chinese Moon Festival

LILY PHONGSA

*T*HE CHINESE MOON FESTIVAL IS the second biggest traditional holiday in China. The biggest traditional holiday is Chinese New Year. The day of the Moon Festival is the fifteenth day of the eighth month of the Chinese lunar calendar. The moon is closest to the earth on the fifteenth day of the eighth month of the Chinese lunar calendar. So, on the Moon Festival day, the moon is very bright and round. It is very close to the earth.

Chinese traditional festivals are usually connected with a legend or story. In China, different cities and provinces have different legends about the Moon Festival. One legend is about praying to the moon. Long ago, there was a girl named Wuyan. Wuyan was an ugly girl at that time. When she was little, she prayed to the moon for help. When she grew up, she became the prettiest woman. She was more beautiful than anyone. The Son of Heaven saw Wuyan on the fifteenth night of the eighth month by the bright light of the moon. Then Wuyan became the wife of the Son of Heaven. In other words, she became his queen. Because of this legend, every year a lot of girls pray to the moon on the fifteenth day of the eighth month.

Another legend is about Chang Er, a beautiful lady living in the moon. In ancient times, there were ten suns in the sky, and the temperature was very high. The Emperor ordered a strong archer to shoot down the suns with his bow and arrows. The archer left only one sun in the sky. Because of his accomplishments, the Emperor rewarded the archer with a pill of immortality, a pill that would let him live forever. But the archer's wife, Chang Er, wished to save the people from his bad disposition, so she took the pill herself. The Emperor was angry and banished her to the moon forever.

The solitary Chang Er was lonely and missed the earth, so every year on the fifteenth night of the eighth lunar month, Chang Er would come to earth to see her husband, the archer. Before the sun rose on the sixteenth day, she would have to go back to the moon. Inspired by this legend, separated couples hope they can be with their spouse on the night of the Moon Festival.

Today most people celebrate the Moon Festival by gathering with their family. Everybody sits outside in the light of the moon with family, dancing, gazing at the moon, and feasting on moon cakes, the special traditional food for the festival.

Chuseok

YUN JU LEE

CHUSEOK IS AN ANCIENT HOLIDAY in Korea. It was originally associated with a month-long weaving contest between two teams. At the end of the day of Chuseok, the team with more woven cloth won. The losing team created a feast for the winning team. Nowadays, on Chuseok, many people return to their hometowns to meet their parents. Most Koreans move to a big city far from their hometowns when they grow up. The ancient traditions and today's Chuseok are different, but the way to spend time with family is the same.

On Chuseok day, in the early morning, the family gathers to hold a memorial service in the honor of their ancestors. After the service, we visit ancestral graves known as *seongmyo*. We visit the graves, cut the weeds, and clean the grave. This custom is a duty and an expression of devotion to ancestors.

Chuseok is a time for rich plentiful harvests. There are many fruits and much newly harvested rice. We make *song-pyeon,* a traditional Korean food, with rice. On Chuseok, we have plenty of rice because this is the time of the rice harvest. On the eve of Chuseok, the entire family gathers together to make *song-pyeon*. According to legend, the person who makes the prettiest *song-pyeon* will have a good-looking spouse or daughter. We enjoy talking while we prepare the food for our family.

I will introduce one additional fading tradition. Mothers and daughters dress in *hanboks*, traditional Korean clothing. They gather around in a circle, holding hands and singing. We call it *Ganggangsulae*, or Korean circle dance. Korean women usually do this for fun. This dance originated from the Joseon Dynasty during the Japanese invasion. At that time, the Korean mothers and daughters dressed in military uniforms and circled mountain peaks. This fooled the Japanese. They thought the Korean military was much larger than it really was. Through this strategy, the Koreans defeated the Japanese. This tradition has almost disappeared in modern times.

We enjoy Chuseok with family members, go to ancestral graves, eat traditional food, and dance with family members. If you have a chance to come to Korea, don't miss the way Koreans enjoy Chuseok and eat *song-pyoen*.

El Dia de Los Muertos

ISAAC CHAVARRIA

*M*Y FAVORITE HOLIDAY IS E l Dia de Los Muertos, The Day of the Dead. The Day of the Dead is a holiday for celebrating our dead loved ones. We remember them every year. In Mexico, we believe souls are still alive after someone dies.

Mexican people have several ways to celebrate their tradition of El Dio de Los Muertos. First of all, as the holiday approaches, people start buying special things. We buy things which the deceased loved ones liked. For example, if some relatives ate spaghetti or smoked cigarettes, we buy the same kind of spaghetti or cigarettes. We cook the best spaghetti. Then we fill a special table with the things for our deceased loved ones.

Then after a few days, we take special flowers to the cemetery. We have three categories of deceased loved ones, adults, children, and close friends. We go to church to give thanks to God for one more day of life and to ask God to receive our loved ones in heaven.

We believe the dead come from heaven and use or eat the things on the table. Finally, we use those things on the table. If the food is still good, we eat it. We smoke the cigaretts and drink the alcohol.

In conclusion, I like this holiday because many people I still love already died. That makes me sad, but every year I remember them again.

A Day for the Living and the Dead
JUAN SAAVEDRA

MEXICANS CELEBRATE THE DAY OF the Dead on November 1 and 2 to honor our relatives who died. Party preparations start a few days before the holiday. The preparations include cooking, making an altar, and cleaning the tombs. All must be ready before the holiday. The altar honors and welcomes the dead. It must have the flowers of the dead, called Cempazuchil. These show the deceased the way home. The altar also includes our relatives' favorite food. It also has water because in our belief the dead will return dirty. They can wash with their own water. The altar has one candle for each dead person. People put toys on the altar for dead infants or children. The altar also has pictures of the dead relatives. The food must be ready before the first of November. We usually put it on the altar by October Thirty-first. People go to the cemetery on November 1 and stay all afternoon at the grave. On November 2, people spend all day. They pray, eat, and play together. This is the day for the living and the dead to share. Some people even like to have mariachi music at the cemetery.

This celebration is one from our Indian people's heritage that Mexicans remember year after year and shall do forever.

The Zapopan's Virgin

ANONYMOUS

In GUADALAJARA, IN THE STATE of Jalisco in Mexico on October 12, we celebrate the Zapopan's Virgin every year. This day is also called Romeria's day. The virgin is the mother of Jesus. Workers and students have this day off because it is also Columbus Day. Consequently, at the same time we have a religious and an historical holiday.

The religious holiday attracts a lot of people from different places across the whole republic to honor Zapopan's Virgin. There is a procession from the principal church of Guadalajara to a church in Zapopan. Zapopan is the city next to Guadalajara. The procession begins at 6 AM at the cathedral. During the procession, people walk and carry flowers and food. It takes four or five hours to walk from the cathedral to the church.

Someone carries a statue of the Virgin in the procession. During this walk, people sing songs for the Virgin and pray for miracles. She is famous for miracles. People usually wear a white shirt or a shirt with a logo of their church. Sometimes during the walk, people feel really tired, so they decide to take a rest for a little while. After people arrive at the church in Zapopan behind the Virgin, a very interesting mass begins.

I have gone to the procession only once. I was in college. For me this was a really exiting experience. I went with all my friends, and we enjoyed that time a lot. As I was walking, I had a little problem suddenly. I had a stomach ache, so I had to stop for fifteen minutes, then I kept going normally. Perhaps that was a small miracle.

Sometimes people use this occasion to have a picnic or a party with their friends. They go with faith and hope for a happy life.

Virgin of Guadalupe
CECILIA HUTSON

IN MY COUNTRY, MEXICO, A big holiday celebration for all Catholic people is the day of the Virgin of Guadalupe on December Twelfth. There is a big festival for all people. Everyone believes in her miracles. They travel like pilgrims from far away to see her image in the church. Some people call her the boss of all Mexican people. She is very famous because of her apparitions. About four hundred years ago, she appeared to some children. Now, one member of each family has the name Guadalupe. It doesn't matter if the child is male or female. The name is Guadalupe.

Pilgrims travel from far, far away. Sometimes they travel for days by foot, by train, by bike, or by car. It doesn't matter which way, but they have to be on time for December 12 at midnight. Everybody gathers at the basilica of Guadalupe in Mexico City to sing a very popular song called Las Mananitas. Everyone sings to her on that day. The very poor people and the very wealthy all sing to her. In Mexico, almost everyone is very thankful to the Virgin of Guadalupe. People ask her to help them when they're sick or when they don't have jobs or money. They ask for all kinds of help. They ask her for miracles or thank her for all the help they already have.

A grand holiday in Mexico for all Mexicans is, without a doubt, December 12, the day of the Boss, the mother of all Mexicans, the day of the miracle, the Virgin of Guadalupe.

Christmas with My Family
ARACELY GODINEZ

CHRISTMAS IS MY FAVORITE HOLIDAY. I love the way we celebrate Christmas in Mexico. A few weeks before Christmas, we decorate the house and the tree. We put other little decorations everywhere. The houses and towns look like Christmas. This day has two meanings. The first meaning is the children's story of Father Christmas. He comes to all the houses on the night of December 24 to give presents. The second meaning is the religious meaning. This is the celebration of the birth of Jesus.

I usually celebrate Christmas with my family. On Christmas morning, I get up early and eat breakfast with my family. After that, I call my aunts, uncles, and cousins to remind them of our dinner invitation and to say Merry Christmas. In the evening, I help my mom to prepare our traditional dinner of *tamales*, *pozole*, and *buneulos*. When our relatives arrives, we all go to church to pray. After church, we go home, and we eat together. We have food and drink and talk with each other. After dessert, one of the adults leaves the table and puts the presents under the Christmas tree. Then we give presents to each other and open our presents. Finally, the children play with their new toys, and the adults sit at the table for a long time talking about the holiday.

I love Christmas because I spend this special day with my family.

Christmas, New Traditions
GREG VALARDE

ON DECEMBER 25, WE CELEBRATE the birth of Christ. Christmas is definitely my wife's favorite holiday, perhaps for a different reason. She goes shopping and decorates the house. For me, the most important thing about the holiday is celebrating it with my family. It is the only time that our family has a chance to be together.

My wife likes to decorate early for Christmas. The first week of December, we buy a Christmas tree together. It takes a long time to select the perfect tree for her. When the Christmas tree is ready, she gets boxes of Christmas decorations from the garage. Decorating our Christmas tree is her favorite Christmas activity. I climb up to the roof to hang Christmas lights. Then I put a robotic Santa Claus and deer in the front yard. My wife and I use our creativity to celebrate Christmas, and we enjoy decorating every Christmas.

My wife loves Christmas shopping. I love celebrating Christmas, but I do not love shopping with my wife. She buys gifts for everyone, and she buys herself a beautiful Christmas dress for the holiday. She goes to every clothing store at the mall in search of the perfect clothes. If she can't find the perfect dress, we go to another mall and another mall, until she finds it. It is a relief when she finds it. This is the moment when I actually thank God for guiding my wife to the clothing store. Christmas is the only time that I go shopping with my wife. She needs me to carry all those packages. It is also the only time I do not complain.

My wife likes to celebrate Christmas at our house with my family. She gives me the list of food for Christmas. Then she goes to Williams-Sonoma to buy Christmas decorations, platters, cups, and tablecloths to decorate the table for our Christmas feast. She makes the formal dining room look very beautiful. It will look exactly like the ones in a catalog. It is very grand but expensive. Christmas is a time for extravagance.

I love celebrating Christmas with my family. Nothing is more special than celebrating Christmas with the people I love, especially if it makes my wife very happy.

Three Kings' Day

IN MEXICO, WE CELEBRATE THE arrival of the Three Wise Men. This celebration takes place each year on January Sixth. The Three Wise Men, the Kings of the East, followed the Star of Bethlehem to reach baby Jesus in Bethlehem. They brought Jesus three gifts: gold, frankincense and myrrh. In Mexico, on this day children receive presents from the Three Wise Men. They do not usually receive gifts from Santa.

On the evening of January 5th, all the children go to bed easily and early. In the morning, they will have a present from The Three Wise Men. They put their shoes next to their bed. During the night, very quietly, the kings put the presents in the shoes or next to the shoes.

In some parts of Mexico, some stores remain open all night. Parents can then buy gifts for their sleeping children. When I was a little girl, I remember the excitement of waiting for Three Kings' Day and having gifts from the kings. My brothers and I went to bed really early. We hoped that the night would pass quickly so we could open presents in the morning.

First, everyone opens presents in the morning. Then the whole family gets together for a feast. For dessert, we eat a special bread called *la rosca* and drink hot chocolate. Mexican hot chocolate has a special taste. It is delicious! *La rosca* is a large oval shaped sweet bread. A little baby figurine hides inside the bread. This symbolizes King Herod killing small children in his kingdom. Mother always cut *la rosca* into seven pieces, and we all grabbed a piece at the same time. The winner of the baby in their piece of bread also has the honor of hosting a dinner in their home on the second of February. This is also a religious day. It is el dia de la Candelaria, the day of the candles.

Now, we live here in the United States. We don't give presents on Three Kings' Day. Instead, we give gifts on Christmas. The tradition is not lost completely. Our family still gets together on the day of the Three Wise Men, and we all still eat the *la rosca* bread. Sometimes, we tell the children not to open one present from Christmas, so that they get to open a present on that day when we eat *la rosca*.

A Special Family Day

GRISEL SOTO

IN MY COUNTRY, MEXICO, WE celebrate many different holidays. One of the most special is Three Kings' Day. This celebrates the day when the Three Wise Men, the Three Kings', visited Jesus. On the fifth of January, every year my family and I get together to honor the birth of Jesus. This is a Catholic holiday. We keep the customs like many Catholic families. My family has the most extraordinary celebration. All the family comes together to pray, hope, and give thanks for the last year and the New Year. First of all, we cook special food for this special event. *Tamales* are traditional. The sweet bread is always on the table. This is special bread only for this celebration.

In my house, we have a nativity scene with Jesus, Mary, Joseph, and animals. We add the Three Wise Men to the nativity on this day. We each put one of the Wise Men close to the nativity. Then we pray for the New Year. After that, we have to dance to traditional music. All the guests put something from the nativity close to Jesus. Then our guests also pray and dance. Usually people pray to thank God for their health and for a good year. It is a nice celebration. There are no gifts. Everyone shows thanks for all of our good fortune.

My grandparents celebrated this holiday with all the family together. The joy came from being with family and friends. On this special day, everyone in my family celebrates together. We talk and enjoy ourselves. We offer our prayers and hopes for the New Year.

Right now all my uncles and aunts and cousins live in different parts of the world, but they still keep this tradition. They are teaching their children this tradition. On this day, we are thankful for one more year. We share our hope for the New Year.

Saint John the Baptist, June 24
RENATO FERNANDEZ

BRAZIL IS THE LARGEST CATHOLIC country in the world. During the year, we have a lot of religious holidays to honor saints. Saint John the Baptist is the most appreciated. This holiday lasts almost one week. I like the holiday because people get excited cooking, decorating the streets, and dancing *forro*.

Saint John the Baptist holiday is the time of corn harvest. Most of the food for the holiday comes from corn. The traditional foods are *canjica, pamonha,* corn, and corn cake. One is more delicious than another. At my house, my mom hires two people every year to help cook all kinds of corn food.

People get together to decorate their streets. The most common decorations are banners crossing the street. They tie one rope and then hang the banners on it. In some cities, they have competition to see which street is the most beautiful.

Saint John the Baptist Day is good because we have traditional music and dance. The name of the dance is *forro*. Couples have to dance together, very close. *Forro* is easy to learn, even people who never danced before can learn it. And it is fun. This dance is romantic. Some dancers find a new boyfriend or girlfriend.

In conclusion, Saint John the Baptist is the biggest holiday in Brazil. It has the name of a saint, but this is not a religious holiday. It is a holiday for fun. People like to cook food from corn, decorate the houses and streets with banners, and dance *forro* to find a partner.

Inti Raymi
LUZ LUGO

I AM FROM PERU, AND THE most important festival is the Inti Raymi. Each year on June 23, the people of Cusco celebrate the festival of the Inti Raymi. This festival was the most important festival of the Inca Empire. Inti was a sun god in the Inca religion, and June 23 was like a new year celebration. It was also connected to the harvest of potatoes and corn. In modern times, there are special foods, music, and plays for the festival of the Inti Raymi. There are also a lot of tourists.

The food for Inti Raymi is delicious. We look forward to this food all year because some dishes are only made during the festival. Many families even create a little restaurant in their homes during the festival. In this way, visitors and tourist enjoy the food, and the family makes some money. This is very important because people from Cusco don't have a lot of money.

The music for Inti Raymi is also special. There are live concerts by the native people. Their music is lively with drums and wooden flutes. All of the musicians of Peru perform during this festival because so many people come to celebrate and listen to music.

The most important event during the Inti Raymi festival is a famous play. It has more that five-hundred actors. They recreate the ancient Inca ceremony. More than two-hundred-thousand tourists come to Cusco every year to watch the play. They watch the history of the Inca become alive during the play. The actors dress in native Inca clothes and speak the ancient Inca language. After the play we celebrate with music and dancing. This is a very beautiful festival. We can meet and become friends with many tourists at the festival. Indeed, the people of Cusco traditionally invite everybody, including tourists, to enjoy this most special day.

After Ramadan
ABDUL ABDULAHMMAD

ℰID-AL-FITR IS THE BEST HOLIDAY of the year for my whole family. This holiday is a heartwarming sacred day for all Muslims. We celebrate Eid-al-fitr after Ramadan. During Ramadan, Muslims fast during daylight hours. They do not eat or drink all day. At the end of Ramadan, Muslims prepare for Eid. People clean the house and make cookies, snacks, and traditional food. All the children and parents go shopping for this sacred holiday. In the morning, children and adults from all ages go to the mosque to pray. Later in the day, family and friends visit each other's homes to express their love and affection for each other. It is also common for children to receive money, called *fitri-roza*, from family and friends. They usually buy toys, candy, or clothes. This money is considered a blessing.

In the evening, people celebrate together until midnight. Some families go to a restaurant and some celebrate at home.

Chaharshanbesuri
KISIA

IRANIAN CULTURE IS FULL OF ancient celebrations. Chaharshanbesuri is one of the most interesting. It is celebrated on the last Wednesday of winter. Nobody knows the origin of this tradition. It started long, long ago with the Persian people. They believed fire is a symbol of purity.

They believed fire could bring positive energy to life and destroy wickedness. This is a celebration of fire from ancient people. In the evening, people gather in one place in each neighborhood. They make several small fires in a row. Then everybody jumps over the fire and sings a short song. At the same time, they wish for good health for themselves during the coming year. The celebration around the fires continues from evening till midnight.

Another part of Chaharshanbesuri is Ghashoghzani. It means "knock with spoon." When the night turns completely dark, young people cover themselves with a thin fabric. No one can recognize them. They go door to door in their neighborhood with a bowl and spoon in their hands. They ring a neighbor's doorbell in silence. They do not speak at the door. Then the owner of the house comes out with some dried fruits or chocolates and candies for them. This part of the event is very similar to Halloween in the United States, but Iranians use fabric instead of costumes.

Another part of this tradition is Falgoosh. It means eavesdropping. An elderly person, the Falgoosh, hides near a corner of the street. No one can see the Falgoosh. Then the Falgoosh listens to the conversations between the people on the street. If the people are talking about positive things, the Falgoosh believes this is good luck for the next year.

Chaharshanbesuri is a purely secular Persian celebration. It has no religious significance. It has no official status in the culture, but it is celebrated gloriously every year.

The End of Life

The End of Life

In Mizo Society
RUATI JOHNSEN

*I*NDIA HAS MANY DIFFERENT CULTURES and customs. We all feel remorse and grief at the end of someone's life. In each tribe the style and traditions are different. I am from the Mizo tribe in the state of Mizoram. The Mizo people are a unique group in India. It is wonderful to be part of Mizo culture.

Mizo society was especially kind and supportive at a difficult time for my family.

My mother was very ill and needed an operation. Several young men went to give blood before the surgery. On the day of the operation, many people came to the hospital to wait with us. They brought tea and food. Many waited with us until our mother was out of danger. Every day visitors came to the hospital to see her. Some people gave us money for medicine.

After three weeks, our mother came home. Nurses came to our house to care for her. Visitors came to offer support for her and our family. Sadly, our mother had internal bleeding. She returned to the hospital, but she died. Members of our community came immediately to form a committee. They made arrangements for the funeral.

We got my mother's body from the hospital and brought her to my uncle's house. There, the nurses bathed her and dressed her. They put her in the coffin and brought it into the living room. The guests were waiting for her. The pastor invited us to pray with him. The family sat in front of the coffin facing the guests. Guests brought beautiful flowers, and soon the coffin was covered with flowers. So many people came. Some had to stay outside. The Mizo committee helped with tables and chairs for them. They also gave them tea. They each wrote their names and kind messages. Many people brought condolence money as part of our tradition.

Everyone from our community went to the cemetery. The community rented two buses to carry everyone. At the graveside, the pastor prayed. He talked about my mother kindly. Finally everyone threw flowers on the grave and slowly walked away. The pastor gave each of us in our family a handful of dirt. My father, my brother, my sister, and I each threw dirt into the grave.

We returned home and found many guests. People prepared food for us. For one month, we had our family or close friends with us. In Mizo tradition, we should not be alone for one month.

The Mizo people honored our family and our mother in her death. She was a member of our community, but in her death she was celebrated like a great visionary.

My Aunt's Funeral in India

ANONYMOUS

SEVERAL YEARS AGO, MY AUNT died very suddenly. The news spread quickly through her town. Soon the priest, well-wishers, relatives, and neighbors went to my uncle's house. They offered prayers and peace for her soul.

The relatives cleaned her body and dressed her in a new white traditional dress. They placed the body with her face toward the east. They put candles, flowers, and incense around the body. The room was filled with the scent of flowers and incense. On the day she died, we had a service for her. This included songs and prayers. Later relatives placed her body in a coffin and carried the coffin to the cemetery in a long procession. At the cemetery, there was another ceremony. Then the priest closed the coffin and the men lowed the coffin into the grave. Then the priest put three handfuls of soil into the grave and said some prayers for her soul. After that, others placed flowers and soil in the grave. Finally the grave was full of soil. That was a very sad moment for us. Many people cried. The priest put a cross on the grave. We lit some candles, and then we went home.

After the funeral, the family cannot cook in the house for seven days. They should eat only simple vegetarian foods. They also cannot go outside during this time. The neighbors bring food and basic necessities for the grieving family.

On the seventh day, we held a small gathering. We went to church and prayed for my aunt's soul. The family continued to have ceremonies for my aunt's soul on the forty-first day after her death, six months after her death, and one year after her death. The funeral is over in two days, but the mourning last for a year.

Traditions in Romania

ANONYMOUS

TRANSYLVANIA, ROMANIA IS FULL OF traditions and
customs related to death. These traditions involve the
separation from the living, the preparation for the other
world, and integrating with those in the world of the dead.

At the end of someone's life, relatives and friends visit
the sick or old person. They ask for forgiveness or offer
forgiveness. They talk about memories and experiences
together. They remember happy times. This makes the
coming separation easier. We also ask a priest to come. The
priest listens to the confession and gives communion to the
dying person.

After a person dies, we pray for the soul to rest in peace.
Then we prepare the body. First, we wash the body carefully.
Then we dress the body in some special clothes. Sometimes
the dying person picks the clothes. We place the body in
the biggest room in the house. All the windows and mirrors
must have black cloth covers. A candle is near the body. It
burns constantly to guide the soul into heaven. Usually, for
two or three nights the body stays at the house. At church,
the bell tolls at midday and at night for three days. Family
and friends come to visit. They pray and cry and show signs
of grief. Everyone prayers for the Lord's forgiveness. The
people from the village call upon the family and stay with
the coffin. Men must remove their hats, and women cover
their heads with a black cloth. Everyone wears black clothes.

During these three days, the family decides about the
funeral. Everyone has a special role. Some carry the coffin.
Some carry the candles. Someone else carries the cross. At
night before the burial, the priest says prayers for the family.
On the third day, they move the body from the house to the

front yard. Everyone comes to say the last goodbye. They go to the cemetery. The priest prays and everyone sings songs.

After the funeral and the cemetery, people go back to the house. Everyone is invited. They all make food to share: wheat bread, stuffed cabbage with meat and rice, and potatoes with fried meat. The priest prays to bless the food, and then we eat.

After six months and after one year, the family has a special celebration and meal together to honor the memory of their loved one. These customs give respect to the dead, and they are a nice way to say goodbye.

A Ukrainian Tradition

ALLA KOTLYAR

IN UKRAINE, TRADITIONS ABOUT DEATH are very special. The family keeps the body at home for two days and two nights. The room with the body is dark. We cover the mirrors and windows. The mirrors and windows can reflect bad memories. Or, bad spirits pass through the glass and can take the spirit of the dead person to Hades. The casket is in the middle of the room, and the lid is open. People put flowers around the casket. The flowers are always in pairs. Pairs of flowers are a symbol or death. People also put important things into the casket. For example, they might put in lipstick, a wedding ring, or pictures. These things can be useful in the afterlife. The lights in the room are always turned off. Only candles can give light. The family is always very polite to each other during this time. They speak in a very quiet voice.

On the third day, the body must go into the ground. The family members and friends all wear black clothes. They take the casket outside. They set it down three time in front of the front door. This is a sign of the final goodbye. Then they take the casket in a procession to the church for the funeral. At church, the parson prays and asks God to forgive the dead person. Everyone prays together with the parson. Then everyone goes from church to the cemetery. They put the open casket next to the grave. Then everyone says good things about the person. Everyone has a chance to talk. Finally, someone closes the casket and puts it into the ground. They fill the grave with dirt. Then the family invites everyone to go back to their home. They all eat a meal together.

We have some other special traditions. If a husband or wife dies, we also have another custom. For example, the wife cuts all of the wedding pictures. She cuts the picture and separates the bride and groom. The wife also wears black clothes for one year. She wears a black ribbon around her head. She can also not watch television for about a year. If an unmarried young woman dies, she is buried in a wedding dress. She might be five years old or twenty-five years old. She wears a wedding dress to her grave. This is a very tender idea about purity and marriage.

These traditions are important for the people in Ukraine.

Vietnamese Funerals
LY LE

$\mathcal{V}$IETNAM HAS A LONG HISTORY and a long tradition for mourning the dead. If a person dies at home, we keep the body at home for at least three days before burial. The family takes care of the person's body. They change the clothes, give a bath, and dress the person for the burial. During these days, relatives and friends come over to see the deceased and the family. They donate money for the family to pay for the funeral. Then they burn incense for the dead person. Everyone sits together to talk about that person. A Buddhist monk will come to the house to pray for a safe journey to the afterlife. We pray for three days. When the monk prays, the family kneels in front of an altar.

We wear traditional mourning clothes and a mourning band. The mourning color in Vietnam is white. Many relatives also wear a mourning band, too. The family does not leave our house. Guests come to us. We can never be a guest in someone's home. Sorrow could fall upon the house if we visit after someone dies.

The time of the burial is very important. It could bring good luck or bad luck to the family. The monk helps us decide the time. Relatives and friends all join us at the funeral. We light incense at the grave and keep it burning for three days.

Three weeks after the burial we have a celebration. We have another celebration after 49 days. The family has a meal together for these celebrations. One year later, we invite relatives and friends to celebrate together. We remember the person kindly. Three years later, it is the end of mourning, and we have another celebration. We burn the mourning clothes and other special things for the dead person. The end of mourning is very important for the family. During the mourning period, we cannot get married or have celebrations. That is the custom.

In Chinese Culture

YUEHUA SHU

I REMEMBER A TIME LONG AGO. My grandmother died. For three days our family welcomed guests and mourned her death. First, they prepared her body. Then they put her in special clothes and put her body into the coffin. The coffin remained open for three days. My family lived together in a large house. Almost all of my father's family lived in that house. That was the custom. In the center of the house was a big room. My grandmother's coffin was in that room for three days. My parents and my aunts and uncles all wore white clothing with a white rope around their waists and heads. During the three days, many people came to visit. Each time someone entered the house, my parents and relatives cried and welcomed the guests.

After three days, eight strong men carried the coffin outside. They walked in a line. Children walked in front, holding a garland of flowers. Someone walked behind the coffin. He held a large basket with special paper. The paper was cut in many different shapes. He threw the paper into the air as he walked. The second person was my uncle, the first son. He held a picture of my grandmother. The adults followed. They each cried and held a stick. Finally, the coffin procession stopped. Then each adult beat the coffin with the stick. They beat until the stick broke.

At the gravesite, I saw a large pit for the coffin. One strong man jumped into the pit. He called the name of each family member and said some kind words to each. Then the person threw money into the pit. After every family member threw money, the man collected the money and climbed out. Then the strong men put the coffin into the pit. They covered the grave with dirt and built a small hill.

That is my memory of my grandmother's funeral.

Thai Ceremony of Death
SIRINAPA CHAISIRINIRUN

IN THAILAND NOBODY WANTS TO talk about death, but I want to share the ceremony of death with you. On the first day after a death, Thai people make a beautiful dress for the body. They take the body to the temple for a special ceremony. They invite family and friends to pour water into the palm of the hand of the deceased. After a day the family will put the body in the mortuary. They send flowers to the mortuary. It will always look beautiful. They then invite monks to pray for the deceased. They come every day to pray at 11 AM and 7 PM. The family must decide how many days the monks will come to pray. Usually they choose three or five days. They never choose an even number. In the evening of each day, the family serves food and drinks for the ceremony. The guests give an envelope of money to the family. It is customary to give money for this ceremony. After three days, the body moves to the front of the crematorium. They have a ceremony of paper flowers. People put paper flowers on a large plate in front of the mortuary. Then the family looks at the body for the last time. We are very careful. We keep tears away from the body. In Thai culture, no tears can drop on the body. The spirits will not be happy. Maybe the spirit of the deceased will not be welcome in heaven. When we go home, we wash our face before we go into the house. Then the body is cremated.

The next day, we go back to the temple after the cremation. We can take the remains back home or leave them at the temple. Some people build a *stupa*, a sacred place, for the remains at home.

We celebrate the life of our loved one at ninty days and then every year. This is Thai culture.

With Prayers and Songs

ROSA E. SUAREZ

IN MEXICO, PEOPLE CAN DECIDE to have the body at home or only in the funeral home. The body stays for twenty-four hours in the home or funeral home. Family and friends gather there to pray. They spend a long time together giving condolences to the family. Friends bring coffee, sweet bread, cookies, or chocolate to the family. Sometimes friends send a mariachi band to sing goodbye to the deceased. They sing the favorite songs and remember the deceased with music. The next day, the body goes to the church for mass. The priest blesses the body. Then everyone walks to the cemetery. The men take turns carrying the casket. Mariachi players join the procession. This is a festive procession. People sing and talk. At the ceremony, we say prayers and the casket is placed in the ground. Then everyone goes back to the home. The next day, the family prays the rosary. They say the rosary and pray the same way for nine days. This is a novena. On the last day, everyone has a meal together.

Funerals in El Salvador
CRISTIAN LOPEZ

IN EL SALVADOR, DEATH IS no surprise. We know that everyone will die, and people die every day. We celebrate the life of the deceased in a most unusual way. On the day that someone dies we have *velas*. For this celebration, the casket is in the yard, and all of the friends and family are there. We eat *tamales*, laugh at stories, and even play cards until five o'clock in the morning.

When my grandfather died, I was sad inside. I was surprised to see people laughing and having fun. I was confused, too. I thought we should act very sad. I learned about *vela* that night. We are poor and had no money for a limousine to take the body to the cemetery. Six people would carry the casket to the cemetery for burial. It is a long walk. They needed *tamales* for strength. They stayed up all night before the long walk. This is the custom. They told stories about my grandfather and remembered happy times in his life. Everyone offered good wishes for my grandfather and our family. I have very fond memories of the celebration. I vowed to show respect to my parents with the same celebration. They will have a *vela*. That is our tradition.

Peruvian Traditions

ANONYMOUS

WHEN MY GREAT-GRANDMOTHER DIED IN 2001, my mother was very sad. Her grandmother took care of me when I was a baby. She told me many loving things about my great-grandmother. We all prayed together for her soul.

In our part of Peru, we carry the coffin from the church to the cemetery after the funeral. Members of the family or friends walked behind the coffin for several blocks to the cemetery. At the graveside, people offered more prayers and said nice things about my great-grandmother.

The next day, many people went to the cemetery again. My great-grandmother loved red roses. They were her favorite flower. In life, she had beautiful red roses in her garden. Many people brought red roses to the cemetery. They put the roses next to her grave. They will bring her peace.

Now, my mother visits the cemetery on the last Sunday of each month. Many other relatives also visit the cemetery to sit by my great-grandmother's grave. They bring her flowers and talk about her life. There are so many other people at the cemetery, too. Many people are crying because they miss their loved ones. This is a tradition in Peru. The streets are full of cars on their way to the cemetery. Many people sell flowers along the way. The cemetery looks amazing with so many beautiful flowers on the graves. Each bouquet of flowers is for someone with love.

Using *One World Many Voices*

Both intensive and extensive reading are important aspects of an ESL reading curriculum. The essays in *One World Many Voices* are designed to provide interesting and easy extensive reading material. They can, however, be used effectively in many ways in the classroom. While extensive reading contributes to overall language proficiency growth and helps students to become successful readers, intensive reading provides instructor-led activities that help students develop reading proficiency and confidence.

Teachers can address factors that lead to unsuccessful and successful reading in the classroom through both intensive and extensive reading activities. Extensive reading alone will not remedy unsuccessful reading practices, but a combination of extensive reading and teacher-led intensive reading activities will remedy most.

FACTORS IN SUCCESSFUL AND UNSUCCESSFUL READING

Factors in Unsuccessful Reading

- Lack of rapid, automatic, and accurate word recognition
- Limited sight vocabulary
- Lack of phonological competence
- Limited grasp of the structure of the language
- Inability to disambiguate information in the text
- Inability to use reading strategies flexibly while reading
- Lack of general world knowledge
- Lack of interaction between textual and general world knowledge
- Rigidity in perception and conceptualization

Factors in Successful Reading

- Rapid, automatic, and accurate word recognition
- Large recognition vocabulary
- Reasonable grasp of the structure of the language
- Ability to disambiguate information
- Ability to establish a standard of coherence, monitor comprehension, set goals, and use strategies to reach that standard
- Ability to integrate meaning
- Ability to make inferences and connections to background knowledge
- Ability to suppress less important information
- Fluency in processing words, sentences, and discourse cues

EXTENSIVE READING

Extensive reading can help second language readers overcome some factors that lead to unsuccessful reading. Guided extensive reading programs provide readers with carefully selected material and suggestions for reading frequency. They promote reading fluency much the way that journal writing helps students become fluid writers. Most significantly, extensive reading provides reading practice. It guides time-on-task for readers who might not be self-motivated.

Material

In order to promote fluency, extensive reading material should be easy to read with few unfamiliar words and easy-to-process sentence structure. Students should be able to read faster than they read for intensive reading and should be encouraged not to use a dictionary. The purpose of extensive reading is general understanding.

The essays in these collections are carefully edited for different proficiency levels of English learners. The vocabulary increases in breadth from the most frequent 500 words to the most frequent 2,000 words in English across the series. The sentence structure also increases in complexity over the collection.

The essays in *Our Cultures* were edited for sentence structure and vocabulary to provide beginning level students with interesting and easy to read extensive reading material.

Each book in the series can provide a portion of the required extensive reading material for one semester. At every level of proficiency, students should engage in extensive reading four to five times a week in addition to the reading they do in class.

The Teacher's Role

Teachers can encourage, inspire, and motivate students to read by engaging in extensive reading along with their students in the classroom and by establishing an expectation of extensive reading outside of the classroom. Teachers are excellent models for reading and discussing books. They can share their own experiences with reading and tell students about the books they are reading. When teachers read the same books that the students are reading, they can share their reactions to the books and guide student discussions. Language learners often have limited experience reading in English or discussing things they read in their new language. The teacher can model these activities and encourage students to discuss their reading with each other.

Teachers might introduce extensive reading with activities that invite students to examine their reading experiences, habits, and attitudes toward reading in their first language.

Goals of Extensive Reading

Extensive reading can help second language readers overcome some factors that lead to unsuccessful reading practices. The goals of extensive reading include the following:

- Improve reading comprehension
- Increase rapid, automatic, and accurate recognition of the most frequent English words
- Encourage incidental vocabulary learning
- Increase reading rate
- Gain overall language proficiency
- Build general knowledge
- Support the development of a reader identity in English
- Establish a community of readers

Suggestions for Teacher-Directed Activities

The essays in *Our Cultures* can be used as a classroom resource not only for extensive reading practice, but also for achieving extensive reading goals. They are a resource for practicing reading skills and strategies that promote successful reading. The following suggestions have emerged from our experience using the essays in the classroom. We hope that you find them useful.

IMPROVE COMPREHENSION

Book discussions can help beginning readers of English develop a sense of competence and autonomy as they read for comprehension. Discussion activities can help them monitor their comprehension and motivate them to develop comprehension strategies. Such strategies include re-reading, looking for key words or ideas, constructing mental summaries, and connecting ideas encountered in the text to their own experiences. Here are some activities that can help learners improve their comprehension.

- After reading a passage once, tell a partner about the passage without looking at the text.
- Read a passage multiple times and tell a partner about the passage without looking at the text. Discuss the comprehension differences after a third or fourth reading.
- Connect the ideas in an essay to personal experience.
- Identify the most important ideas in an essay.
- In pairs or small groups, discuss an essay in light of similarities and/or differences with personal experience.

LEARN AND PRACTICE READING STRATEGIES

Students learn reading strategies from their reading textbooks and practice applying those strategies during teacher-guided activities in class. The essays in this book can provide additional practice opportunities for mastering those strategies and for supporting their integration into students' independent reading practices. Here are some activities that can provide learners with opportunities to practice various reading strategies.

- Ask students to preview the book and discuss its overall organization as a class.
- After reading a chapter, ask students to work in pairs or small groups to draw inferences about one or more of the essays. For example, students might be asked to draw inferences about cultural expectations or values not explicitly discussed in an essay.
- Ask students to discuss their previous knowledge or experience with a topic from one of the chapters. For example, ask students to tell about a unique cultural tradition.
- Ask students to scan for particular information. For example, students might scan a passage for key words or ideas.
- Select one essay in a chapter and ask students to look for transition signals, key words, or other coherence devices that link ideas from within and between paragraphs.

INCREASE READING RATE

Slow readers spend a great deal of time processing individual letters and words, making it difficult for them to understand what they are reading. Reading faster will aid comprehension and increase reading pleasure. It will also contribute to overall academic success. English language learners will naturally increase their reading speed over time as their general language proficiency increases, but with practice and guidance their reading speed can increase more quickly. Here are some activities that can help students increase their reading speed.

Reading Pairs

1. Select a passage from the book. Ask students to work with a partner.
2. Partner A reads aloud for 30 seconds.
3. Partner B reads the same passage for 30 seconds.
4. Repeat.
5. Ask how many more words were read each time.

Reading Sprints

1. Select a passage from the book. Ask students to read silently for four minutes. Use a timer or a watch with a second hand. Then ask them to count the number of lines they read.
2. Students then count out the same number of lines in the next part of the passage. They continue reading for three minutes, trying to read the same number of lines in less time. Students count the lines they read in three minutes, count out the same number of lines in the next part of the passage, and try to read as many lines in two minutes.
3. When the reading sprint is complete, the class can discuss their comprehension of the text.

Monitor

1. Encourage students to monitor their reading speed.
2. Have students chart their progress.

RAPID, ACCURATE, AUTOMATIC WORD RECOGNITION

Increased reading comprehension and reading speed are only possible when students can rapidly and accurately recognize large numbers of words in print. Their vocabulary for listening and speaking is not accessed for reading unless they also recognize what a word looks like on the printed page and then connect that word to their mental lexicon. Extensive reading exposes language learners to the printed word, but it does not ensure that students accurately process the correct meaning. Some read aloud activities can help language learners connect printed words to the vocabulary they have developed for listening and speaking. It can also provide consistent pronunciation practice.

Read Aloud

- After students read a passage silently twice, ask them to read it aloud to a partner.
- Assign one paragraph of a passage to each student. For homework the student should practice reading aloud, focusing on careful pronunciation and phrasing. In class, students read to each other.

Pronunciation

- Encourage students to use the computer software or Internet interface of an English language learner dictionary and ensure that students know the pronunciation of the a large number of the most frequent English words.
- Encourage students to say and write words to promote the connection between the written and spoken forms.
- Make pronunciation an important part of knowing a word.

ENCOURAGE INCIDENTAL LEARNING AND DEEPEN WORD KNOWLEDGE

Sometimes students believe that reading will help their vocabulary development only if reading texts contain many new words. Talking to students about the value of reading easy texts for learning vocabulary may help them see the value of extensive reading more clearly.

Extensive reading can also help students deepen their knowledge of known words since knowing a word includes many types of knowledge such as knowing the spelling, pronunciation, and multiple meanings of the word. Simple activities such as reading aloud, listening and repeating, and listening to audio files of passages can all contribute to deepening learners' knowledge of a word. Teachers can also direct students' attention to words in a passage that draw on less frequent uses of those words.

LINK READING AND WRITING

Regular journal writing about topics from their reading can promote both reading and writing fluency. Ungraded reflective writing about their ideas after reading promotes close reading, encourages readers to explore reactions to the text, gives them a chance to examine features of a text more closely, and encourages readers to link their own experiences to those of the writer. Here are some possible journal prompts.

- What does the author mean by...?
- How are the experiences of the authors different from or similar to your experiences?
- What did you think about as you read...?
- What was interesting/confusing about this essay/chapter?
- Write about your own wedding or about a wedding you attended.

INCREASE OVERALL LANGUAGE PROFICIENCY

Listening, speaking, reading, and writing in English all require knowledge of grammar. Reading easy and interesting material, as students do with extensive reading, helps them confirm their knowledge of English grammar and provides extensive input upon which to make further generalizations about English grammar. Here are some activity types that can help learners gain overall language proficiency.

Sound-Spelling Relationship

· A student whose native language uses a writing system that is very different from the English alphabet will likely benefit from activities that focus attention on sound-spelling relationships.

· Copying a paragraph can give students easy practice with forming letters and spelling.

Grammar Analysis

Analyzing the grammar in a passage helps students to focus on language structure and to discuss their observations. Each activity should take no more than 15 minutes. The possibilities are endless, but here are some ideas.

1. First, select a paragraph that has a sufficient number of the target structure and make an overhead transparency of the paragraph.

2. Students should first work alone for three minutes to identify as many examples of the target structure as they can.

3. Next, ask students to work in pairs to confirm their findings.

4. Finally show your own findings on the overhead. At the beginning level, students benefit from identifying the subject, verb, and period of each sentence. They can identify noun phrases, prepositional phrases, subject phrases, and verb phrases. They can find pronouns and articles.

DEVELOP FLUENCY

Reading fluency and speaking fluency often develop at different rates. When students have opportunities to talk about what they are reading, they bring together multiple skills. The activities below also encourage integrating reading and speaking skills as well as multiple readings of a text, which can deepen understanding and enable readers to see something new with each reading.

Read Aloud

Students should read a passage silently multiple times and rehearse before reading it aloud to a partner.

Oral Summaries

Students retell passages from memory and confirm comprehension.

1. Students read one entry as many times as they can for 10 – 12 minutes.
2. With a partner, retell/summarize the passage.
3. Identify key points with the whole class.
4. Read the passage again.

Summary Sprints

In pairs, students summarize a passage.

1. Student A has three minutes to summarize the passage.
2. Student B has two minutes to summarize the same passage.
3. Student A has one minute to summarize the same passage.

BUILD GENERAL KNOWLEDGE

Each chapter in *Our Cultures* includes both personal experience and information about the writer's culture. This diversity of experiences provides geographical, cultural, religious, and family perspectives and provides an opportunity for readers to develop knowledge about cultures and countries very different from their own. They can confirm their new knowledge through discussion activities or research assignments.

ENGAGE IN CRITICAL THINKING

Students need practice thinking and analyzing as they read. Some simple activities that encourage students to think about organization of ideas and how ideas relate across several essays can help students to do this on their own. Here are some examples of how to use the book to encourage critical thinking.

- Each chapter in the book focuses on a particular set of cultural experiences. Select several passages about the same topic, and ask students to work in small groups to identify some similarities.
- Encourage students to draw conclusions from reading about a particular cultural tradition. Ask critical thinking questions such as why a particular experience was important to the author, what aspects of the experience reveal something about the author's culture, or what the author does not express that might be important.
- Ask students to select their favorite essay from a given chapter and to tell a group of students the reasons for their opinions.

SUPPORT READER IDENTITY IN ENGLISH

Developing an identity as an English reader over the course of several semesters can help language learners transition from learning to read to reading to learn. Extensive reading provides the time-on-task that builds confidence, promotes learning, and provides practice. All of these can lead to increased pleasure reading, other types of independent reading, and related oral or written activities that readers engage in as part of what it means to be a reader. Activities that invite students to discuss or write about their experiences as English readers can help them be more aware of their development of an English reader identity.

CREATE A COMMUNITY OF READERS

Many of us have had the pleasurable experience of talking to friends and colleagues about a book we have read. When we discuss our own reading with others, we become part of a larger community of readers. When language learners engage in reading the same book as part of their extensive reading, they have the opportunity to experience that same pleasure. They share their ideas and participate in a community that values reading and sharing ideas about that reading.

Countries

AFGHANISTAN
ANGOLA
BOLIVIA
BRAZIL
CAMBODIA
CHINA
COLOMBIA
EL SALVADOR
ETHIOPIA
GHANA
INDIA
INDONESIA
IRAN
JAPAN
KOREA
MEXICO
PAKISTAN
PERU
POLAND
ROMANIA
RUSSIA
SERBIA
TAIWAN
THAILAND
UKRAINE
VIETNAM

Index of Authors

*M*ARILYN MARQUIS TEACHES ESL AT Las Positas College in Livermore, California. She was inspired to become an ESL teacher after hosting two young people through the Experiment in International Living. She began teaching English as a Second Language at Long Beach City College in 1983 and was an adjunct English and ESL teacher there until 1991 when she joined the faculty at Las Positas College. Reading instruction has been an area of particular interest to her throughout her professional life. She has enjoyed the collaboration on this series of student-generated essays. Marilyn holds a bachelor's degree in English from California State University, Northridge and a master's degree from California State University, Dominguez Hills.

*S*ARAH NIELSEN HAS BEEN INTERESTED in language learning and teaching since she was a high school student. She spent a year in Belgium living with a French speaking family and attending school before she began her university education. She taught English in China for two years before entering graduate school. She began teaching as an adjunct ESL instructor in 1995 before joining the faculty at Las Positas College in 2000. In 2004, she joined the faculty at California State University, East Bay, as the coordinator of the MA TESOL program. Sarah holds a bachelor's degree from the University of California, Santa Cruz, and both a master's degree, and a Ph.D. from the University of California, Davis.

CPSIA information can be obtained
at www.ICGtesting.com
Printed in the USA
FSOW01n2247250716
22940FS

9 781595 944115